Stolen Water

Also by W. Hodding Carter

A Viking Voyage Illustrated
A Viking Voyage
Westward Whoa!

Stolen Water

Saving the Everglades from Its Friends, Foes, and Florida

W. HODDING CARTER

ATRIA BOOKS

New York   London   Toronto   Sydney

ATRIA BOOKS
1230 Avenue of the Americas
New York, NY 10020

Parts of this book have appeared in *Smithsonian* and *Outside* magazines.

All interior photographs are courtesy of Russell Kaye.

ISBN: 0-7434-7406-6

First Atria Books hardcover edition July 2004

10   9   8   7   6   5   4   3   2   1

Interior design by Davina Mock

For information regarding special discounts for bulk purchases,
please contact Simon & Schuster Special Sales at 1-800-456-6798
or business@simonandschuster.com

Manufactured in the United States of America

To Anabel, Eliza, Helen,
Angus, and Lisa

Contents

Contents

Stolen Water

Manateeville

I AM SITTING ON A DERELICT PIER OUTSIDE OF MELBOURNE, Florida, babysitting a dead manatee. It's one of those grimy mornings, where you're caked with sweat and smog by 10:00 A.M., and frankly, I'd like to be elsewhere— like sitting in the sand, a tall mango smoothie in one hand, the latest Harry Potter in the other, my kids frolicking in the surf. Instead, I'm here on the other side of paradise, watching a manatee decompose.

This particular manatee, recently found floating in some retired couple's backyard, has just been dragged a mile through the Intracoastal Waterway while tethered to a marine patrol boat. Skin is sliding off the poor thing as though it were a blanched tomato, and it smells like forgotten, one-month-old hamburger meat in the back of your fridge. This poster animal for the Florida environmental movement isn't going to make it to the kind of photo shoot you'd prefer.

All in all, it's an unpleasant beginning to a close study of Florida's ecology.

Two teenage boys, having seen me disembark from the patrol boat, ask my permission to swim. I glance down at the manatee, tied by its tail to the closest piling. Oily fluids slowly mushroom from the decaying body into the murky waters, and the Intracoastal looks as refreshing as a festering sewage ditch. "Sure," I say, shrugging my shoulders. "Why not?"

A marine patrol officer brought the manatee and me to this spot about a half hour earlier, bitterly complaining about spending three hours out of an eight-hour day on a dead animal. How can he do this while effectively enforcing the no-wake manatee zones? So upon my suggestion, he's left us alone to wait for a state marine biologist.

A sign declaring HAVE DEAD MANATEE, WILL TALK must be hanging over the dock because as the teenagers tentatively enter the brown muck, a skinny worn-out alcoholic teeters over from his broken-down pickup truck. "I've never seen one of these before," he declares, his Adam's apple bobbing up and down like a freaked-out aquarium fish, his breath drowning me in sweet fermented fumes. "I've always wanted to. I love wildlife." He peers down, nearly losing his balance. "It's not doing so well, huh?"

"Yeah, this cold water, even though it's only in the mid-sixties, is pretty rough," I offer, passing on information I've only just learned myself. "It kills them, even."

"This one's not dead, though. Just hurting a bit, huh?" The odor of decay is about to make me barf. After I break the news, the besodden sireniaphile stumbles away, head shaking. "Oh, I wanted to see a live one. Never seen one of them."

I understand how he feels. The reason I was in Florida was to see a very special live manatee named Brutus. My youngest sister had adopted him for me on my birthday, coughing up twenty dollars to the Save the Manatee Club, a nonprofit protector of *Trichechus manatus*. The West Indian manatee, indigenous to the West Indies, Central America, and Florida, isn't doing so well, although humans have been trying to protect them as far back as 1764, when Florida was briefly an English colony. "His majesty (proposes) that an Instruction should be given to the Governor of the Provence of East Florida," declared a representative of King George, "to restrain him from granting to any person whatsoever, without His Majesty's particular Orders and directions, those parts of the Coast of the said Province frequented by the Animals called the Manati or Sea Cow, where they have their Echouries or Landing Places."

Of course, everyone ignored this and Florida eventually became the developer's Mecca that currently makes it the fastest growing state in the nation. And as far as the manatee itself goes, humans continued to hunt the poor bastard to near extinction until it was placed on the endangered species list in 1973. Today, it's not faring much better, especially when compared to fellow endangered classmates like the bald eagle and the wolf, both of which were recently delisted. There were only a few thousand back when the manatee was first classified as endangered and today there are still only an estimated three thousand.

What do Brutus and his fellow *Sirenia* (the manatee's order) have to do with the Everglades? Well, pretty much everything. I've come to believe that as the manatee goes, so goes the Everglades. Their past, their fate, and even their range are intertwined. Look at one closely—how it lives, where it lives, and what we do to help it live—and you've looked at the other. The manatee also serves as a primer on Florida's environmental management programs. The mammal's traditional habitat was the Everglades and its surrounding waters, and development has pushed both the Everglades and the manatee to the brink of extinction. And if we really protect the Everglades, then we'll probably end up protecting the manatee far into the future, or vice versa. So, we begin with the manatee.

The day Brutus's adoption packet arrives I don't know all of this, of course. Instead, I'm just wondering what silly thing has my sister done. Who has *time* to care about manatees? is all I'm thinking. Glancing at the club's literature, I learn that they only mate every two to three years and their gestation period lasts three months longer than a human's. Multiple offspring are nearly unheard of, and they have a high infant mortality rate. Their cousins, the Steller's sea cow, were hunted to extinction centuries ago. Florida's manatees are threatened today because they live in the shallows of both fresh- and saltwater, where pollution and development destroy their habitats. Boats hit them all the time. Well, that's awful, I mutter, and begin wondering how best to remove gum from my daughter's hair. But then something about Brutus's sad face and sunken eyes catches my attention. He is, after all, family.

As I read on, I notice that Brutus, probably in his late thirties, is very close to me in age. He likes to swim; I like to swim. He eats nearly 200 pounds of hyacinths and other water plants a day; I've been known to eat a lot, too, although I've never tried a water hyacinth. He weighs nearly 2,000 pounds; I weigh 165. He is quite the ladies' man, always seen chasing the girls; I, well . . . But what is this? According to the literature, Brutus is often found sleeping by himself. Is he depressed? Bitter? Suffering a midlife crisis since manatees only live to sixty? Suddenly I decide we have to make sure he is okay. "Brutus, we're on our way! Don't you worry!" I call out, speaking also for my wife and three daughters. "We'll swim together. Take some pictures. Let you meet your sisters. Make you feel like part of the family. Everything is gonna be all right!"

Before heading down to Florida, I figure I need to talk to Jimmy Buffet. I've noticed he co-founded the Save the Manatee Club in 1981 with then-Governor Bob Graham, and I figure he'll have a word or two to pass on to Brutus. I call his publicist, whose blunt response strikes me like a whirring propeller (the average manatee is hit by boat props up to twelve times a year, according to one informal study). "Jimmy is not available to participate. He is only making himself available for national television programs." Undeterred, I have her submit some questions anyway. "Do you have any message you might want to give Brutus or any of the other manatees you're helping to save?" I ask, and "Do you know anyone who might have been a manatee in a former life?" The publicist gets back to me a few days later and says Jimmy isn't answering the questions, not even the one asking how he might begin a song about manatees.

Hell, even I can do that:

Manateeville
Nibblin' on eel grass,
Watchin' some mare's ass;
All of those big boats loaded with Bud.
Swimmin' to warm springs, listenin' to props zing.
See our backs!

They're covered with blood.
Wasted away again in Manateeville,
Searchin' for our lost celebrity friend.
Some people claim that he'll bring us to fame,
But we know, this is surely our end.

Well, hopefully not, but things do look dire for the manatee, despite the efforts of the Save the Manatee Club and a cobweb of federal and state wildlife agencies. Between the club's adoption program and the state of Florida's Save the Manatee license plates and various other fund-raising efforts, millions of dollars are spent each year on rescue efforts, government research projects, and educational programs (for humans, not manatees) from Florida to the Carolinas. It's an uphill battle, against such well-connected foes as Wade Hopping, lobbyist for the National Marine Manufacturers Association, who a few years back called for the species' delisting because the manatees, he said, had made such a great comeback. Hopping speaks for boaters who don't like the no-wake and no-boat zones posted in high-density manatee habitats. Meanwhile, the manatee's mortality rate has slowly been increasing. (Three hundred and five died in 2002, and boats caused one-third of those deaths.) You don't have to be a pathologist to figure out why. A manatee's rib bones are solid and heavy, not porous like ours. When one of these bones is broken by impact, say whacked by an overloaded Ski-Doo, it's like having a hardwood two-by-four snapping apart inside you and splintering right into your heart, lungs, liver—anything vital.

Luckily, Topping and his cohorts haven't won yet, and in a few of the no-boat zones, the manatees are doing quite well. Brutus's wintering grounds, Blue Spring State Park, is among them.

Back in 1970, when motorboats were still allowed at Blue Spring, only eleven manatees basked in its warm, calm waters, which fed the equally languorous Saint Johns River. Now, more than a hundred gather there each winter. Many scientists believe there are three distinct Florida manatee populations, although all are of the same species: the East Coast manatees, whose range stretches from Miami up to the Carolinas; the West Coast manatees, who travel from the Keys as far west as Alabama, and the Saint Johns. The main Saint Johns attraction is Blue Spring itself. Fed by ground-water seeping through limestone bedrock, it remains a constant 72 degrees: manatee heaven.

That springwater sounds inviting, but I am told swimming with the manatees is a no-no. "We consider it harassment," Nancy Sadusky, spokeswoman for the Save the Manatee Club, explains. Detecting my disappointment, however, she hastily adds, "You can still take Brutus's picture if you see him."

Blue Spring State Park is thirty miles northeast of Orlando, and as we make our way there, my wife, Lisa, and I try to prep our kids about Brutus and his friends. While driving down McDonald's-Exxon-Comfort Inn-Jiffy Lube Lane in Orange City, about to turn off for the park, Lisa tells the kids that Brutus, like most manatees, can be identified by the propeller scars on his back and that Brutus has a couple of big ones. "Why do the boats cut Brutus?" asks Eliza, then four. Because the boats go too fast in shallow water, we answer.

Anabel, her twin, chimes in. "Is Brutus better?"

Yes, yes, we say. Helen, our wise two-and-a-half-year-old, holds her own sage counsel, staring mutely at her manatee book.

"But the boats might cut his back again, huh?" Eliza continues.

We arrive at the spring before we have to answer. "Bruuuuutus!" the girls yell, running to the boardwalk that hugs the spring's shore. "Where are you, Brutus?"

A lush hammock of magnolias, live oaks, and pines engulfs the bank, making it nearly impossible to see the spring except at a few cleared overlooks. The girls pry their way past dozens of baffled tourists staring blankly at the vividly clear water at the closest viewing area. But there's nothing to see except a few fat catfish and a small school of tilapia. Brutus, along with all the other manatees, is nowhere in sight.

The park allows visitors to swim in a section of the spring each day—just not near the manatees—and half a dozen people are already splashing around the narrow waterway. Human-manatee interaction isn't a problem because, understandably, the manatees have left. Park rules state that if a manatee were to reappear, everyone would have to get out of the water. (Fat chance, unless there's a ranger around.) As a result of this open-swim policy, the manatees head back into the sixty-degree (or colder) river every afternoon, traveling perhaps dozens of miles for food and with any luck, a shallow pocket of warm water. Most manatees get cold stress at anything below sixty-eight degrees. Prolonged exposure to the cold water causes internal infections and canker-like sores, similar to frostbite, on their extremities. This often leads to death. Knowing this, the park tried to squash swimming a few years back, but bowed to political pressure after divers complained to their state legislators.

We wait around, hoping against hope that Brutus might show, despite the swimmers. Besides my concern for him, I don't want to have come all the way from Maine for nothing. But hours pass, and no Brutus. Dejected, we set up our tent in an RV site at the park, since no tent sites are available. Thirty miles northeast of Orlando might be a great place for manatees, but it's a little less so for humans. The area's sprawling development is as inescapable and frightening as the giant strip mall that stretches all the way from Orlando. During our entire stay at the state park, beeping, churning construction equipment serenades us wherever we go. The 3700-acre park makes a poor holdout in the fight against overdevelopment.

Later, while our girls are pouring topsoil over each other, Lisa suddenly blurts out that the tourists are depressing; Blue Spring gets up to two thousand visitors a day because of the manatees, and we've seen people dropping trash all over the park grounds, chasing great blue herons, and generally causing a ruckus. "They're a blight on this beautiful setting," she adds.

"What makes us any better?" I ask, slightly defensive. After all, I've dragged her and the girls down here on my whim. A seemingly befuddled, foot-long box turtle walks by.

"We're not. We're a blight, too. We should all commit mass suicide."

Our friends Russell Kaye, Sandi Phipps, and their daughter, Lucy, join us a little later at our campsite. Russell and Sandi have come to photograph the manatees, but suffering from a family-sized case of strep throat, the three of them are no boost to our sagging morale. We go to sleep early that night to the sounds of a fellow camper's radio.

The next morning, after temporarily putting off a mutiny to abandon Blue Spring and drive over to the Gulf Coast to see the mermaid show at Weeki Wachee Springs, Russell and I accompany park ranger Wayne Hartley on his daily head count, while our families watch the manatees from the boardwalk. The air temperature is a cool fifty degrees, mak-

ing it a good chance Brutus has turned up. When I ask Hartley about the chances of a Brutus sighting, he says that Brutus does return to Blue Spring every year, as my brochure had claimed, but he only stays for a few days at a time and then disappears for weeks. "It's got to be really cold to keep old Brutus in," he says.

A big man but not quite man-atee big, Hartley has been monitoring the annual winter retreat to Blue Spring for twenty years.

We paddle just a few yards past the no-boat zone (marked by PVC piping stretched across the mouth of the spring) and hover over a bunch of manatees. It is extremely underwhelming. They look like sunken fat cactuses with sparse bristly hairs dotting their bulbous backs. Eventually one slowly rises to the surface, just inches from our boat, revealing its stoppered snout, making me suddenly giddy. It is so close; it might be Brutus. The nose unplugs and a reverberating exhale, similar to the spouting of a small whale, echoes across the still waters. Its breath smells a bit like a deflating tire, only mustier.

"Brutus?" I ask.

"No, that's . . . Phyllis," says Hartley. One hundred and thirty-one manatees have come up to Blue Spring this winter, and he and various scientists have named nearly every one of them.

Another and another and another rise around us. Soon dozens of exhaling cactuses surround our canoes. (That's really how they look from overhead.) I haven't expected it to be like this, great clumps of them floating beneath us as we paddle overhead. Manatees are supposedly solitary creatures, but scores have rendezvoused at the spring's warm mouth, conserving their energy by letting the waters keep them warm. Calves nurse for up to two years, but one mother not only has her one-year-old close to her side but also a pair of older adoptees vying for nourishment.

Hartley begins a running dialogue with his friends that doesn't stop until we are back on shore two hours later. "Glad to see you, Floyd. . . . There you are, Jax. No, you're not Jax. Wait—yeah, you are, tail buried in sand." Half of Jax's tail is missing, perhaps from a run-in with fishing line. Next to boating accidents, entanglement is the single biggest cause of injuries. "There's Georgia," Hartley continues, taking pictures and recording distinguishing marks while he talks. I half-expect him to give each manatee a friendly slap across the back, he reminds me so much of a politician courting his constituents. "Third year back. Great success story. Picked up at sixty-three pounds. Six years at SeaWorld, released here." Georgia looks to be at least fifteen hundred pounds, if not more. "Problem is that Georgia likes people too much. She's even tried to climb steps out of the run to follow someone. She's taught her calf Peaches to like people, too." Hartley sweeps his paddle over the water, indicating the whole lot. "The brats, I could beat them all." Peaches, by the way, is a boy. You can tell the differences in sex by the proximity of the genitalia opening to the umbilical scar and anus. Males' are closer to the umbilical scar, females' to the anus. (Of course, the manatee must roll on its back for you to see this.)

One manatee takes a shine to me and won't leave my end of the canoe, nuzzling up to me, trying to touch my hand. "Oh, that's Unknown Eleven," Wayne says, glancing over his shoulder, noticing a tail scar. Finally I silently touch its head, unable to resist. According to the manatee-human interaction rules of the U.S. Fish and Wildlife Service, this touching is okay because the manatee has approached me, but the park does not condone such behavior.

Unknown 11's skin is rougher than I thought it'd be, almost like sandpaper. The manatee comes back for more—clearly very fond of me. I begin to believe that there's this simpatico thing between us, but Hartley says this behavior isn't unusual or safe. "The more they like hanging around people, the more they hang around boats and thus the more they get hit," he cautions.

I ask if Brutus is like this. Wayne laughs. "Naw," he said. "Brutus is a real manatee. He moves away from the canoe, if he is awake. He is very calm, laid back, though."

We see seventy-two manatees this morning, but no Brutus.

That night during dinner at an Olive Garden, about the only place in town that serves salad, I get more grief, not only for keeping us in central Florida but seemingly also for the whole manatee situation. "I wish they didn't give the manatees names," Sandi says. "What's with calling him Brutus? Or Louie? It anthropomorphizes them. It's kind of weird, don't you think? It makes you want to pet them."

Ashamed, I don't mention touching Unknown 11.

Brutus does not show up the following day, either. It is just too warm, with the air temperature in the seventies and eighties during the day and only the low fifties at night. Weighing roughly a ton, Brutus, and most of the older manatees, have little need for Blue Spring. So Russell and I head over to Melbourne on the Atlantic Coast to watch a "manatee recovery," while our families go see some mermaids at Weeki Wachee on the Gulf Coast.

And that's how I end up babysitting the dead manatee. The manatee and I sit there for another half hour watching the teenagers contract tetanus before Ann Spellman, a biologist for the state-run Florida Marine Research Institute, arrives with Russell in her manatee rescue/recovery trailer. All recovered manatees are given a necropsy to determine age and cause of death, and once we have this young male loaded up, Spellman decides to perform the postmortem right in the parking lot behind her office. The nearest pathology lab is three hours away, and she has to hurry to an afternoon meeting (where she will be told that her already-meager budget is being cut).

"The first thing I like to do is cut the head off to get it out of the way," Spellman explains, as scores of flies swarm around her and the manatee. It is the seventh of January and already this is her fourth postmortem of the year. She is squatting inside the partially enclosed trailer, which has a slick fiberglass coating so it can be easily hosed out. A pervasive stench clings to anything within a dozen feet. Apparently breathing through her nose as well as her mouth, Spellman immediately slices through two layers of fat and muscle. Two more quick strokes with her poultry knife ("It has a good long handle," she says) and the manatee's head is severed from its spine. The head slides a few inches on its own fluids and stares out the van in understandable disgust. "At least he's not a slimer," she says. Evidently, slimers have been rotting for even longer than this pup and are named for obvious reasons.

Pointing out puffy white sores on the animal's flippers, tail, and head, Spellman initially thinks it has died of cold stress. Dozens of barnacles cling to what is left of the manatee's skin, which has peeled off from decomposition, but there are no signs of recent boat scars.

Spellman slices through half a foot of meat and finds swollen lymph glands and other signs of infection that support her initial evaluation. Seeing the manatee cut up, it no longer seems so surprising that these animals cannot handle what seems like relatively warm water. Although there might be a foot of meat between skin and internal organs, there is shockingly little insulating fat, less than an inch in thickness, so little as to make a seal die of laughter. Russell, for example, has plenty more fat than a manatee.

As Spellman studies the cadaver more closely, though, she begins to notice odd things—a bloodred liver that should be brown, a collapsed left lung. Then she realizes two ribs are out of place. She turns the animal on its side. An ugly white scar that we hadn't seen earlier stretches across its back. "Boat," she says and then starts digging around the ribs more hurriedly. Turns out there are six fractured ribs from the impact. Judging from its size, Spellman guesses the manatee to be a two-year-old, perhaps still nursing. I ask her if this doesn't upset her. "I love animals, but it's like I'm a fireman," she says. "You don't see a fireman bawling his eyes out at the scene. You start bawling your eyes out while watching a stupid schlocky movie, not here."

Spellman cleans up the mess, stores the head to be sent off to a bio lab (where its exact age can be determined by growth rings in the ear bones), hauls the carcass to the land-fill, and heads off to her budget meeting. Since it is still extremely hot out and Brutus is nowhere to be found (I've checked with Wayne by phone), Russell and I rush across-state to catch the mermaid show.

Lisa, Sandi, and the girls have already seen the morning performance. "They've got a summer mermaid camp," Lisa gushes when we arrive. "Their makeup stays on even when they're underwater. You should see how they hold their breath."

"Do they look anything like manatees?" I ask. Supposedly, sailors, long at sea, started the mermaid myth by thinking manatees were women with tails. Christopher

Columbus was the first historical source for the connection, and all he wrote was that the mermaids (which were really manatees) were not quite as handsome as artists had portrayed them over the years.

"No," she continues unflustered, her face flushed. Evidently, she's discovered her next career. "But to become a mermaid all I have to do is be able to hold my breath for a few minutes underwater while changing costumes. . . . Did I tell you Elvis is here?" Back in the early sixties Weeki Wachee was hip: Don Knotts, Elvis, and lots of people I'd never heard of made it to the hourly shows. To this day, Elvis can still be heard over the loudspeaker.

The show, a musical rendition of *The Little Mermaid*, is mesmerizingly awful. How do they get that makeup to stay on? One of the mermaids slides right past the underwater glass, and personally, I can't see how the mermaid/manatee myth ever started. These mermaids at Weeki Wachee look nothing like manatees. To begin with, manatees' breasts are found under their front flippers, and that certainly isn't the case with the Weeki Wachee mermaids, and the lack of said flippers sort of negates the argument, too.

"They're so cute," the woman behind us says at the show's conclusion.

Well, manatees are cute, too, but in a different sort of way.

While you can barely even look at a live manatee at Blue Spring, the wild and woolly West Coast is a different story. That night we stay in a trailer home at the Marine Park Inn on Homosassa River a few miles up from Weeki Wachee. A huge billboard out on the road says SWIM WITH THE MANATEES. This we have to see.

We rent a pontoon boat the next morning and slowly

waddle up the river toward its source—another warm spring, and the reason for the hundred or so manatees that convene on cold winter days. Not far from the mouth of the spring, nearly twenty tourist-choked pontoon boats and more than a hundred snorkelers are packed in an area half the size of a football field. It is manateemania. Not only are these people swimming with the manatees, but they are also rubbing the manatees' bellies and backs. Some people even look as if they're trying to have sex with the poor beasts. Others, like part of a hunting party, are chasing down retreating manatees, desperate not to let them get away.

There are no law enforcement people around and there never are, according to two hapless Manatee Watch volunteers, who paddle up next to us. When they see something unlawful happening, the volunteers approach the swimmers and discourage them from breaking the law. "We feel the manatees are being harassed by the dive boats, but there's nothing we can do," the woman tells us. A few minutes after we speak, the volunteers do successfully break up a gang of people that have separated a mother from her calf. Mostly, though, the volunteers just paddle along, caring but ineffective. The U.S. Fish and Wildlife officers in this area only give out half a dozen tickets for harassing manatees in a given year, and in five minutes we've witnessed about seventy infractions. Where are those guys? Some of the tour boats are not obeying the no-wake zone, and their captains certainly aren't discouraging their paying customers from breaking the rules—they smile distantly as snorkeler after snorkeler harasses a fleeing manatee.

"Hey," one particularly goofy snorkeler yells out, "he's got my hand with his flipper and won't let go! He really won't." Take him down, I plead silently. Take him down. A woman wading nearby says, "They're so cute."

To be fair, some of the manatees are clearly attracted to the boats and humans. Lisa, Russell, and Sandi get in to take pictures and one or two manatees approach them. The manatees perform headstands and even nudge them with their noses to get scratched and petted. Whether this is true affection, or simply a result of years of being hand-fed lettuce by misguided tourists is hard to tell. I jump in, too—like everyone else, I just have to get a look from underwater. It's not often you get to be within inches of a wild animal, you say to yourself. "See, we're not all bad," you're thinking as it gets closer and closer. Then, you reach out and . . . another manatee is dead.

My reverie is broken. What the hell is going on here? This is an endangered species. Back when bald eagles were on the endangered list, you couldn't even possess one of their feathers. People aren't supposed to touch endangered species. Boats shouldn't be able to motor up to an endangered species and then drop dozens of ignorant tourists in their laps. There shouldn't be signs on the highway exhorting people to swim with the endangered manatees. Go swim with a Weeki Wachee mermaid! What is the State of Florida doing to these poor animals? What is the U.S. government doing?

Hell, why not let people feed them, take them home as pets, shoot them even? I've read that the meat tastes pretty good; people still poach them to this very day. Soak their tails in brine and have a party! It doesn't really matter. They're not going to be around much longer anyway, except in aquariums and zoos, if Florida keeps developing at its current rate.

So I'm just about to touch the one swimming up to me, when I wake up and kick my feet madly to scare him away, hop out of the water, rev the engine as loudly as possible, and happily see a few manatee splash down to deeper, safer water.

* * *

The next day Lisa, the girls, and I return to Blue Spring, still hoping to catch a glimpse of Brutus.

We paddle into the wide, coffee-colored Saint Johns from the mouth of the hot spring. It's a dark river, stained with tannin, and it seems unlikely that we'll see any manatees, let alone Brutus. It is a Sunday and dozens of boats motor up and down the river; only a few are disobeying the no-wake zone.

Occasionally one of us calls out, "Brutus!" scaring up egrets and herons but no Brutus. Once we startle a twelve-foot alligator snoozing on the northern bank, and the creature scurries directly toward us. Alligators don't eat manatees; the lummoxes are just too thick for their jaws, but they have been known to eat a young child now and then, so we casually suggest to the girls that they stop paddling for a minute.

Finally, when enough mosquitoes have bitten us and the girls are scanning in all directions for attacking alligators, I stand up in the canoe.

"Daddy, don't do that," Anabel says. "You said we're not s'posed to."

I explain this is a special case. I'm planning to make one last plea. Perhaps I started out as a deadbeat adoptive parent, but now I truly care. I want to be there for him, the adopted son I've never known. But something profoundly different comes out of my mouth. "Brutus!" I yell. "Don't come back! We're not worth it!"

Brutus does come back, of course. A few weeks later Wayne Hartley e-mails to announce his return. Like all manatees, he needs that warm water. Brutus has been coming to Blue Spring for thirty years and he probably will continue to do so until the day he dies.

I hope I never see him.

Go Away, Go Away, Go Away . . .

THE FACT THAT THE STATE OF FLORIDA AND THE FEDERAL government were horribly mismanaging something as simple as a bunch of John Goodman–sized, slow-as-salted-snails sea cows got me wondering. How might things be going elsewhere, with the state's bigger environmental projects? And that's when the words *the Everglades* popped into my head like one of those brilliantly lit "south of the border" billboards. That place had to be an ecological nightmare. How many times have they "saved" it so far? Two? Three? Four?

A little bit of research revealed they were, in fact, going for another "save" under something called the Comprehensive Everglades Restoration Plan. After my manatee experience, anything touting itself as "comprehensive" regarding the combination of Florida's state government, the Feds, the natural environment, engineering, and restoration was like a platter of sushi set before a coked-up table of 1980s-style Yuppies. Iraq laid out before Donald Rumsfeld. A pot of succulent gumbo, simmering with arrogance, corruption, ignorance, and vainglory, waiting to be devoured by a roomful of starving Cajuns.

The state was staked out in the clarifying, inescapable light of the subtropical sun, just waiting, hell, beckoning, for someone to swoop down and announce all of its exposed faults. Or something like that.

Right now water dribbles into the lower half of the Everglades like so much waste from an old-man manatee's bladder. It's polluted, inconsistent, and painful.

And like old age, this should come as no surprise, even to the most casual observer of Florida's history. For more than a hundred years—from 1850 to just a few decades back from now—the state of Florida waged war on the Everglades. Its citizens had mistaken this somnolent river for a swamp and draining swamps fulfills an age-old uneasy covenant between men and the Judaeo-Christian God—a God-sanctioned recovery from the Flood, if you will. Keeping their end of this unspoken agreement, Floridians casually set out to drain some 4 million acres, dynamiting dozens of waterways, scoring South Florida with a thousand miles of canals, raising seven hundred miles of levees, and damming, stopping-up, and squeezing-dry everything between.

After spending tens of billions of private, state, and federal funds, the state finally won this war back in the 1970s. More than a million acres had been claimed for development. Flooding was controlled; the cities had fresh water and farmers could irrigate year-round.

At the same time South Florida's population had increased twelvefold, skyrocketing from 500,000 to 6 million since 1948. Developers created megalopolises on teeming wetlands. Sugarcane farming, practiced on what used to be the upper Everglades, grew from a pipe dream to a business that generates more than $2 billion a year in sales and employs nearly 40,000 people, seemingly half of them lobbyists in Washington, D. C., and Tallahassee, the state capital.

The old Everglades was gone forever. In its place, ironically enough, sat a series of languishing, interconnected swamps.

The Everglades had been swamped.

As a result, most of the water that used to flow so gently across this deltalike landscape—1.7 billion gallons of it—is dumped into the Atlantic Ocean and Gulf of Mexico every day. One-point-seven billion gallons every day—an amount made even more unpalatable by the fact that even when South Florida suffers daily water shortages from recurrent droughts, this water still goes unused. As these 1.7 billion gallons make their way through the canals toward the oceans, uncountable pollutants from sewage, agricultural runoff, and outright criminal contamination join the flow, altering Florida's coastal waterways to such a degree that the U.S. mainland's largest living coral reef in the Florida Keys National Marine Sanctuary is fast becoming America's largest dead coral reef. (Not everybody knows this, so keep it under your hat for now.) Meanwhile, 90 percent of the Everglades' wading birds have disappeared, and extinction threatens more than five dozen species of animals—from the Key Largo cotton mouse to the Florida manatee.

A few years back, a significant portion of Florida's *Homo sapiens* decided it was time to respect the lives and homes of other species. Over the preceding years most Floridians had watched the animals and birds of the Everglades engage in some serious, involuntary family planning, find somewhere else to live, or simply give up and go the way of the dodo—bye-bye birdies—without shedding a tear. But suddenly they didn't want that anymore. After spending all that time turning a unique river into a swamp while thinking that they were actually draining a swamp, therefore creating exactly what they were trying to get rid of in the first place, they wanted to turn it back into a river. And so now does the federal government.

Under direct orders from Congress to restore the ecosystem, a suddenly environmentally aware Army Corps of Engineers—along with the South Florida Water Management District (SFWMD), the U.S. Park Service, the Fish and Wildlife Commission, university scientists and professors specializing in either the Everglades or related studies, and many other agencies and environmental organizations—spent more than six years in the 1990s developing a new plan for the Everglades. In 2000 Congress accepted the Corps' work and passed the Comprehensive Everglades Restoration Plan as part of the 2000 Water Development Act. Interestingly, the Corps had labeled their initial water-control plan for South Florida "comprehensive" back in 1948, complete with multiple drainage ditches and dikes, when they came up with the best way to maintain South Florida's ecosystem, but the second time's the charm, right?

Under this new plan, dams will be exploded, roads elevated, and some 240 miles of levees and canals will be removed and filled in, respectively. All to improve the flow of the Everglades, resuscitate all these endangered animals, and provide even more water for crops and people. The project will cost at least $8 billion—half of which will be paid by the U.S. government, the other half by Florida—making it appear to be the biggest restoration effort in the world. The plan is supported by hundreds of disparate organizations—from environmentalists to developers—because it will provide more water to the depleted Everglades, to all the thirsty farmers whose land once used to be a part of the Everglades, and to each and every grass-loving suburbanite with a green lawn in South Florida. Instead of being dumped into the ocean, much of the water will be pumped 1100 feet underground into the Floridan aquifer at 333 sites around the Everglades under a new system of wells called Aquifer Storage and Recovery. Then, when needed, the water will be retrieved and supplied to the cities and farms. Their wastewater and runoff will be scrubbed clean and pumped into the Everglades, via new and improved ducts and canals.

The Everglades will be restored and everybody wins!

That's a good one, the naysayers snarl. The people who oversaw the Everglades degradation in the first place, the Army Corps of Engineers, still control the tap. Critics remind us that the new plan, termed a "restoration plan" by Congress, was merely called the Comprehensive Everglades Review Study by the Corps; the Corps didn't intend to restore the entire system. At best, the Corps's plan is only about protecting what's left while providing enough water for agriculture and the cities. Why else would conservative Republicans and Democrats fall over each other to sign on to the Comprehensive Everglades Restoration Plan (what everyone refers to as CERP, but I'll call "the Comprehensive Plan," since I have an aversion to acronyms)? Everybody in Congress voted for the plan, tree-huggers and road-pavers alike, except one lone Republican senator from Oklahoma. Why? Because the word *restoration*, critics claim, is just a smoke screen. The Everglades isn't going to be restored, just helped a bit.

This may sound like semantics, but there is a crucial difference between restoring and saving. Perhaps the public, the media, and many of the politicians who voted for Everglades restoration don't know that *restoration* is a term of artifice—some politico's spin on what turns out to be just another water management project. But since the word *restoration* has been used, people believe that's the goal. The Everglades will be restored to a pristine river of grass. Casual environmentalists are appeased, and conservatives, pointed to the fine print, can see that development and agriculture are protected more than ever. Many in Congress believe it's real restoration. Maybe even Presidents Clinton and Bush did; their press releases and speeches certainly give that impression.

But are the naysayers correct? Is the $8 billion Comprehensive Everglades Restoration Plan a boondoggle? Why should we even care whether or not it gets restored? What is the Everglades? Why does it have a *the* in front of it? Why is it called a "River of Grass"?

So *Outside* magazine, coaxed on by my claiming I'd paddle the ninety-nine-mile waterway on Everglades National Park's western border to expose the real Everglades, sent my photographer friend Russell Kaye and me back down there to find out what was going on. Why would they back such a ho-hum endeavor? I told them we'd travel *sans* food—live off our natural instincts and all the Everglades still had to offer. It would be a hoot.

The only problem was that the Everglades itself, a nearly indefinable ecosystem sprawling with polluting farmers, bickering environmentalists, competing scientists, thieving capitalists, and most important of all, a touch of nirvana, hadn't figured into my smug musings. It was only meant to

be a tool for investigating Florida and the federal government. I hadn't figured what would happen if the Everglades
actually meant something to me, if it actually affected me.
And if you spend enough time in the Everglades, the one
thing it'll do is mean something to you.

Day 1. Arrive in Miami. Plans unraveling. An Everglades
National Park ranger has left a message on my cell phone.
She says we can't forage in the park but are free to fish as we
canoe through the mangroves, if we have licenses. Russell's
left a message saying he's sick and probably isn't going to
make it. My local hospital back in Maine has lost my blood;
the very blood that might show how polluted the
Everglades is—if we catch enough fish and crabs. Mercury
levels in Everglades fish are seven times higher than levels
deemed safe by the EPA. My quasi-scientific idea being that
if Russell and I eat a lot of contaminated fish, it'll show up in
our blood with an elevated heavy metal count. We'll be living proof that the Everglades needs even faster help.

Outside the airport, newish hotels are being ripped down
to make way for more runways. The Miami River rapids
used to ripple right through this area, crowded with oaks
and pines, saw grass and arrowroot, deer and heron whose
screams and calls pierced the thick, sweet air. Then, in the
early 1900s, the aptly monikered Florida Governor Napoleon
Bonaparte Broward waged war on the Everglades; it was his
entire campaign platform in the gubernatorial election.
During one of the skirmishes, he ordered the Miami rapids to
be bombed and dredged out of existence. Sure enough, they
were dynamited to smithereens in 1909. Now the water
trudges by as a canal, choked by water hyacinths, hydrilla,
and abandoned cars—some, no doubt, with murder victims
in their trunks. Airplanes and cars deafen the skies; motels,

gas stations, and topless bars crowd the paved roads. It seems a little hopeless, this goal of mine to expose the heart of the Everglades.

What a contrast to a hundred years ago when Hugh Willoughby, a late-nineteenth-century adventuring dilettante, prepared for a trip across the Everglades by practicing poling his canoe up the Miami River to this spot.

"The river winds in beautiful curves, the trees growing to the water's edge, and were it not for the occasional cocoanut-tree or cabbage-palm, you would almost imagine yourself in one of the wild streams of the Maine woods," Willoughby marveled. "Very soon we saw large white objects ahead, which proved to be balls of foam hurrying down with the current. . . . We were on the falls and how the water did run! I could hear Brewer [Willoughby's guide] panting beside me but I never turned my head or gave any signal that we were conquered, but started in on my old-time stroke, inch by inch crawling up that water, dodging the rocks. After about three quarters of an hour of the hardest paddling I think I have ever done, the water slowed up a little and we could get some speed on the canoe. The trees opened up more, the stream becoming narrower and narrower, until we came to an opening where everything was clear ahead. This was the edge of the Everglades. The stream here loses itself among the lily-pads and before you lies a sea of apparently pathless grass."

Driving into the city, I know Florida is regretting the watercourse it chose many years ago. It's late March 2000. I scan the brittle landscape and *The Miami Herald*. Parched by its worst drought in decades, the land is drier than a bowlful of Grape-Nuts. Swamps have turned into baked fields. Alligators are invading homeowners' backyard pools and ponds. Garden-clubbers are secretly watering their lawns at night. And the nearby Everglades is fast becoming the Neverglades.

I spend my first afternoon swimming in the twenty-yard pool at my dad's high-rise condo along Miami's booming Brickell Avenue, waited on by immigrant Ecuadorians posing as Cubans, loosening up in the poolside hot tub drinking bottled water, mindlessly watching water gush out of the marble fountain, and, a little later, recovering from my exertions by lounging in the steam bath on the penthouse floor. Turkey vultures, riding the arid thermals conjured up by the fifty-story monolith, glare at me through two-story tall windows as I step into the upstairs whirlpool. I can't help thinking they look thirsty.

Day 2. On my way to Everglades City to meet Russell, if he shows up, and a recent addition to our party, Tad Pole (not his real name). Tad's deceased uncle was my sister's husband. He lives nearby and is just going to paddle with us for the first day.

Drive through Little Havana, grabbing a cafe cubano, liking the scene: old men shuffling by in their guyabarras, dark suited younger men grabbing a con-leche, workmen flirting with the smiling bakery clerk. This is 7th Street, start of the Tamiami Trail. It's not an Indian name, just Tampa and Miami squashed together. The trail will lead me to the historical heart of the Everglades and is all most people ever see of the nation's largest wetland. Part of an urban sprawl unequaled anywhere else in America, the build-out forces me to take forty-five minutes to cover twelve miles. Latin bodegas blend into car dealerships, shady storefronts hiding imagined drug dens, and then adult bookstores. Abruptly strip-mall America appears: Blockbuster video stores, Publix grocery stores, McDonald's, Taco Bell, Wendy's—all surrounded by colonies of newly built ranch houses with stamped-out stucco walls and red clay roofs—a mass-produced facade of tropical living: a developer's wet dream and a preservationist's nightmare. Shortly after passing beneath the Florida turnpike, this, too, disappears. Spread out before me like a Hollywood-ordered set are head-tall cattails and saw grass, on both sides of the roadway and seemingly forever. There's no neutral zone separating the diametrically opposed factions of development and the wild. Nature and Commerce caught in a stare-down. Who's gonna blink first? Up to now, it's always been nature.

An Army Corps of Engineers canal parallels the roadway, broken on occasion by sluiceways and small locks used to maintain a safe water level that is determined thirty miles away to the north at the Corps's Lake Okeechobee headquarters. A couple of tank-shaped boats with meshed-steel front-end loaders plow the waterway, lifting out ton after ton of vegetation, an occasional car, and anything else that might hinder the water's flow, including the infrequent bullet-ridden body. The canals that crisscross the old Everglades are great not only for draining unwanted water but also for disposing of unwanted people: expendable business partners, upstart drug dealers, and argumentative spouses. The South Florida Water Management District, the organization charged with maintaining all the canals below Orlando, discovers dozens of bodies a year in the canals.

Back on Tamiami Trail, it takes about two hours to reach my destination—Everglades City, a squat, pallid little town bloated with trailer homes and pickups overshadowed by improbably tall sabal palms—to rent canoes and register our trip with the park. Carved out of the wetlands back in the early 1920s as a get-rich-quick scheme, Everglades City apparently never got rich. Imagine that: a town surrounded by pestilence, surly natives, and life-sucking mosquitoes, and it didn't catch on. A certain Baron G. Collier, advertising executive from Memphis, Tennessee, who believed in living up to his name, bought a million acres of the Everglades from railroad and timber companies that had stripped the Everglades of anything they thought worthwhile, mainly cypress and royal palms. This made him the largest land-holder in the state, Master of the Everglades, and in 1923 the Florida legislature named the entire area Collier County. It was his personal millions that completed the Tamiami Trail in 1928—dredged and pounded into existence to bring in the tourists, settlers, and small-time developers to Ever-glades City and the surrounding area. Hardly a single inch of square ground in Everglades City is natural. In the mid-dle of this "swamp" Collier built a town hall with a Greek facade and planted his ostentatious palm trees. He laid out the streets as if it were Paris, but the grandiose plans col-lapsed, finished off when Collier lost his fortune during the Depression.

I've been here before but still feel unnerved by its frontier-like quality. The cheerless streets, the scrawny tat-tooed guys milling around the gas stations, and the preda-tory gaze of the shopkeepers remind you you're on your own. More than a few people eye me as I drive by, perhaps wondering if I'm just another serial killer—ever notice how many serial killers are based in Florida?—or better, a com-peting drug runner. Back in 1983 nearly half the town's pop-ulation of five hundred was arrested for drug trafficking. Maybe they just think I'm another fisherman. The town watches thousands of fishermen come through every month from November to April, with hardly a one spending more than a few bucks in the local stores.

It wasn't always like this. After Collier's money dried

up, real Floridians stayed and created a temporarily solid community. When John Rothchild, former editor of the *Washington Monthly* and author of the Florida memoir *Up for Grabs*, moved here back in 1973, the typical family could claim three generations of Florida residency. "These fishermen were friendly, polite, reserved, and straightforward; honesty did not seem to be a symptom of mental retardation with them," Rothchild recorded. "They waved at us from their pickup trucks and waved at each other with each pass—the town's one square mile supported wavers in constant motion. When they weren't waving from trucks, they were waving from crab boats, which the men docked along the Baron River. The Baron River led through a bay and a labyrinth of small islands to the Gulf of Mexico."

About the only thing I can see in common with Rothchild's Everglades City and this present place is the Baron River. Oh, and the ridiculously wide streets that were supposed to look like those found in Paris's city center. Not a single person waves to me the whole time I'm here.

I get our camping permits at the park's visitor's center down by the water on a flat plane of land that owes its existence to Collier's dredges. The ranger reminds me that we can't forage and that many of the fish are weighted down with mercury. Here's the warning put out by the park: "High levels of mercury have been found in Everglades bass and in some fish species in northern Florida Bay. Do not eat bass caught north of the Main Park Road. Do not eat bass caught south of the Main Park Road more than once a week. Children and pregnant women should not eat any bass. . . ." How many bass can you eat if you don't know where the Main Park Road is? We're also not supposed to eat these fish more than once a week: spotted sea trout, gaff-topsail catfish, bluefish, jack crevalle, or ladyfish.

After checking in at our outfitter's hotel and setting up canoe details, I'm hungry for a better sense of the Everglades. Thanks to Peter Matthiessen's *Killing Mr. Watson* and the memories of a previous trip I'd taken with my wife in the early nineties, I've always thought of the Everglades as nothing more than a brackish outpost, haunted by mangroves, migrant birds, and forgotten outcasts. Now, after a few weeks of scientific journals and ecological tomes, I know the Everglades is much more—that it's a "river of grass" with hammocks of subtropical life scattered about, for instance— but what does this mean? How does it feel? Is Everglades City the real Everglades? I hope not.

Having a few hours before Tad or Russell shows up, if he's going to show up at all, I drive north on the only other road besides the Tamiami Trail. A canal lines this highway as well, but after a very short while, the scenery gives way to massive citrus fields and sugarcane plantations—they're all you can see in any direction. Eventually I find myself in Clewiston, U.S. Sugar's company town that sits low and dry behind Lake Okeechobee's thirty-five-foot-tall Hoover Dike. A road sign proclaims Clewiston AMERICA'S SWEETEST TOWN, and as I cruise down the main street, watching dark gray smoke billowing out of U.S. Sugar's new refinery, I like Clewiston more than Everglades City, despite an oppressive gloominess, which is sort of like preferring death by burning at the stake to being drawn and quartered by horses. First of all, the place has real Mexican restaurants, but more to the point, nobody's staring at me and the hair doesn't stand on the back of my neck as I get out of my car at the local hospital to have blood drawn. (I won't feel this way on subsequent visits when nobody will talk to me unless the conversation's been cleared by the public relations folks at U.S. Sugar.)

The hospital receptionist, wearing a miniskirt and low-cut top doing obvious battle with the drab, frumpy clothing of the technicians and nurses who whisk by, doesn't hesitate when I tell her I want to have some blood drawn for a heavy metal test, even when I tell her about my mostly joking theory that Russell and I might eat so many fish and crabs that our lead and mercury count will skyrocket.

Taking my theory as some sort of cue, she tells me how boring Clewiston is. I think she invites me over to her house, but I'm not sure because just as quickly, she launches into what appears to be a heretofore privately held conviction: The sugarcane industry is causing cancer. She leans in conspiratorially, nearly forgetting to breathe between sentences.

"You're just the person to tell this to. You've got to look into this, okay?" I nod my head. "Haven't you noticed? This place stinks. My husband says I go on and on about it too much, but I can't help it. This place is the stinkiest place I've ever lived." She's touching my forearm, although she's not even the nurse. Her voice drops to a near whisper. "Someone needs to look into this." She looks around. A clerk and a nurse are rolling their eyes, but she doesn't seem to notice. "Don't tell anybody I told you this, but children are coming in here with cancer like you've never seen! And they're covering it up. I know this nasty place is killing us. I refuse to go outside when they're burning although they say it's okay. Where are you staying tonight?"

A nurse pulls me away, but I tell "Erin" I'll look into it.

Afterward, inspired by this encounter with a would-be whistle-blower, I careen my rented Impala off the highway, bounce over a stretch of dirt road, and come to a dust-clouded halt on private property. Feeling a little 1970s' Bob Woodwardly, I hop out of my car and grab my prey with a mighty jerk. Nothing. I tug again, and get leaf-cut in the palm of my hand, but I come up with a five-foot sample of purported evil: *Saccharum officinarum.* Noble sugarcane. After tossing it into the back of the car, I grab two handfuls of soil, too. I've never seen anything so black, except the time I was knocked out riding my Schwinn with the groovy monkey bars and banana seat back in second grade. I can see why wars have been fought over this dirt, and still are. I drop both handfuls into a Ziploc.

On my return to Everglades City, red ants, roused from the sugarcane, bite my ankles. (Sometime later, when I'm back home in Maine, I look into Erin's concerns and to my surprise find that the Clewiston area actually has lower rates than the rest of the state for most cancers. But the sugar industry doesn't get off that easy. The Clewiston area does have the highest rate of diabetes.)

Back at the motel, Tad is the first to show up. For the past few months he's been sending me information about swamp cabbage—what stores label "hearts of palm"—because before the park put the brakes on my foraging plans, swamp cabbage was going to be our staple. I can't quite figure out why he wants to join us.

We sit in our cramped, paneled motel room, getting high—me, the first time in nearly a decade—exhaling in front of a puny fan aimed out the window. Tad gives me an old copy of *Travels of William Bartram,* first published in 1791. "Do you know Bartram's Travels?" Carlyle once asked Emerson. "Treats of Florida chiefly, has a wonderful kind of floundering eloquence in it; and has grown immeasurably old. All American libraries ought to provide themselves with that kind of book; and keep them as a future biblical article."

Bartram never made it into the lower Everglades, but he did venture near its headwaters. Traveling up the Little

Saint Johns, he described marvels in a manner that makes you want to read each one independently, pause, imagine what he was seeing, and only then continue on—read him as leisurely as he seems to have traveled with his local Indians and white settlers. "Behold the watery nations (schools of fish), in numerous bands roving to and fro, amidst each other; here they seem all at peace; though incredible to relate! But a few yards off, near the verge of the green mantled shore there is eternal war, or rather slaughter. . . . Yet when those different tribes of fish are in the transparent channel, their very nature seems absolutely changed; for here is neither desire to destroy nor persecute, but all seems peace and friendship. Do they agree on a truce, a suspension of hostilities? Or by some secret divine influence, is desire taken away? Or are they otherwise rendered incapable of pursuing each other to destruction?"

In my present state his words seem inspirational. Haven't things always gone better for me when I've laid everything out in the open? Shouldn't we always try to stay out in the clear stream? It seems an appropriate book to begin this trip with.

I want to hug Tad but hold back, reminding myself that I'm high. Why would he need a hug from me? Am I gay? (Pot makes me paranoid.)

A little later Russell shows up. He's with his wife, Sandi, and daughter, Lucy. He's just returned from a photography assignment in Cuba and between trips to the bathroom—Castro's revenge, he calls it—he still claims he isn't going with me. At the moment I don't really care. In my marijuana-induced haze I'm having a hard time remembering what he's saying, what I'm saying, or why it matters. I'm not even sure where Tad has wandered off to. He's standing beside me one minute and gone the next.

Later, during dinner, Russell flip-flops and says he is, after all, going on the trip. He must be high, too.

Day 3. Sweetwater Bay chickee, southwestern Everglades. Crouched on the pressure-treated boards of our sleeping platform, Russell stares at the dead shark in the encroaching darkness, hoping something will come to him, perhaps some voodoo incantation that will kill me and end his misery. However, the shark isn't giving up anything except a cloud of suffocating, humid odors that engulf us as the corpse thumps against the hull of our canoe. We found the shark already dead a few miles back when lost amongst the mangroves and tugged it behind our canoe with hopes of using it as bait. Almost losing it, I begin breathing only through my mouth.

"Can you catch blue crabs at night?" Russell finally asks when it's clear the shark isn't coming to his rescue.

"Yeah, but I'm too tired to cook," I answer. "It'd just be a waste."

"That's okay. I'll eat them raw." He doesn't make a move, though. We've paddled twenty miles, and though we've only been without food for one day, having caught no fish along the way, something about the exertion, the open-water effort, and perhaps foremost, the eeriness of the waterway makes the situation seem worse than it is.

We have packed a map and compass, but without the park service's marker posts we would have been lost and dead eighteen miles back. Navigating the bays and inlets that crisscross the murky water is like being five again, searching for your mother in a department store the day after Thanksgiving, thwarted by thousands of legs. The hauntingly identical mangroves and indiscernible passages wreak havoc on your psyche.

"I shoulda taken that Captain's Platter in a doggie bag. I've started on a deficit, you know," Russell continues, referring to his purported dysentery. His verbal tempo builds into mania and I inch away from him. "But I bet that curry paste'll taste good mixed in with some water. So what did you bring for a snack? Ha, ha, ha, ha. I need a snack. I need some carbohydrates. I'm not really hungry. No, no, no. I just need a scrambled egg. Hey, I got it. Let's do that trick where you put a light in the water and attract baitfish. I'd eat baitfish. No problem. This is more a trip of the mind than anything else, huh?"

Admittedly, I've been thinking a similar thing—about how I viewed the Everglades differently when reading Peter Matthiessen on the beach, sipping lemonade and eating potato chips. In such a circumstance, it is easy to disregard passages about panthers swimming up and eating someone's goat and the book's general tone of gloom and foreboding. Matthiessen's book romanced me. This, however, is different. This is real. Maybe attempting to traverse the ninety-nine-mile waterway without bringing along food isn't such a bright idea after all.

I feel the mangrove jungles—a mere ten feet behind us—beckoning, the sirens of the Everglades. Their danger alluring, their leaves trembling in the breeze, they appear to be simultaneously beckoning and advancing toward us, the prop roots stepping closer, closer. Climb in here and end your troubles, they croon. Twist your leg in our tangled mat, fall flat on your face, and never be heard from again as crabs, no bigger than your eyeballs, devour everything but your bones.

A delightful invitation, yes, but I've got the blood of Odysseus coursing through my veins. The ropes of commitment bind me to our quest. I resist the mangroves' song, choosing instead to embrace our self-inflicted suffering. We'll see just how far we can make it, just what our limits are—perhaps even what the Everglades itself is made of.

Right now the score may be Everglades–1, Us–0, but I'm not giving up. And I know that despite his moaning, Russell isn't giving up, either. His heart is turning toward our battle. Look, he's lying there peacefully, not a worry in his head.

At which point Russell, on his back, perfectly still, says to no one in particular, "I hate the Everglades. All it is is a bunch of brown water, brown tree trunks, and green leaves. There's nothing else here."

Infidel.

"I want to go home," he adds, and turns away from me onto his side.

Tad's slumped against a post, sketching. Earlier, he found a dried-up Cuban lizard. He's strung some fishing line through it and is wearing it around his neck as a fetish. I'd had no idea how fast this place would affect us.

I'm reminded of a cautionary story David Herndon, our canoe outfitter, had told me the day before. A while back he rented two canoes to three young guys from the East Coast. They'd set off full of life, loaded with ice chests chock full of beer and tasty treats. They had seemed as capable as any of the other thousands of people who've paddled the ninety-nine-mile waterway in the past fifty years. David was supposed to meet them in Flamingo, the waterway's terminus and the only town at the bottom of the park (or on the mainland adjacent to Florida Bay, for that matter). When they didn't show up, he set out to find them, searching the route of the itinerary they'd registered with the park. About fifteen miles north of Flamingo, he spotted them. Two were in one canoe, paddling toward a chickee. As he approached, David couldn't see the third man. The two-manned canoe was towing the second canoe. "What happened?" David asked, coming in closer. "Where's the third guy?"

"Back there," one of them said, motioning to the other canoe. "We had to tie him up. He went crazy. He started ranting a couple of nights back. Tried to walk out of here." The third man was indeed back there, hog-tied and silent.

I'm guessing there was a look in that miserable guy's eyes, a wild, frightened, primordial stare—a look we were just beginning to appreciate.

Day 4. Almost within reach of Onion Key Bay. Tad's gone. He paddled off in the wrong direction without a chart after we ate a hand-sized snapper for breakfast. I hope he made it back home.

It's three-thirty in the afternoon. We've covered about eight miles and have three to go before we get to a campsite on an old mound called Lostman's Five. The mounds—anything more than a foot or so above sea level in this part of the Everglades—are all man-made. When you step ashore, you're stepping on an archeologist's manna. They are kitchen middens, garbage dumps, really, built up by the Calusa Indians over centuries of tossing out bones, shells, broken pottery, and other refuse. They even buried their dead in these middens. The Calusa were the only people who have ever known how to live in this place on its own terms. They didn't grow a single crop, just ate what was there. It seems every speck of dry land is a clue to unraveling the mysteries of the Everglades.

We're resting in a shady cave of red mangrove limbs in the winding stream between Plate Creek Bay and Lostman's Five Bay. Red mangroves, the salt-sucking omnipresent ankle-breaking creeps, aren't even red—unless you cut their bark. Then, they bleed a bright, vibrant rose. They produce nothing consumable by humans, but in the past, between their roots, they harbored fledgling fish and growing shrimp. Now, though, thanks to poor water management and pollution, the fish and shrimp are disappearing—a tragedy I feel personally since I've brought my shrimp net along. All we've eaten for thirty-six hours are three blue crabs and a dinky eight-ounce snapper, split between us for breakfast. Russell isn't speaking to me, or maybe I'm not speaking to him. I'm finding it difficult to think clearly. And right now I'm so tired I can't even raise my arms to paddle. I make a few feeble efforts but quickly give up. I don't need them anyway; we're not going anywhere. Some waterbugs skitter past. A couple of crows are laughing at us. Even in my weakened state I do notice, though, that there aren't anywhere near as many birds flying overhead as I'd seen with Lisa eight years earlier. No swallow-tailed kites soaring casually overhead. No brilliant flock of roseate spoonbills. Not a single green heron. Just the mocking crows and an occasional great blue heron. Lisa and I saw so many birds the first time we couldn't even keep count.

Russell and I are trying to decide whether we'll head to Watson's Place tomorrow and forage for food or try another mound some Outward Bound friends have told me about. I remember from my trip down this waterway with Lisa that Watson's has lots of cultivated plants gone feral, but it's pretty exposed there. There's a much better chance the park will catch us foraging, even though I've been told they let Outward Bound forage on some of the mounds. Also, at this point, I hate Peter Matthiessen. I'm blaming him for getting me into this mess, with all his evocative writing. I want to skip Watson's.

Suddenly a man and a woman zip around the closest S-curve. In their fresh, new inflatable boat, they sparkle in the dappled light like a pair of angels.

"Hey, how y'all doing?" Russell casts out, perhaps with his last breath, his voice quavering and defeated.

They slow down, not hooked, but certainly interested. They ask us the same.

"Fine, fine," Russell mumbles, "if you like starving to death. I'm Russell, this is Hodding."

Snagged by his melodrama, they cut their motor. They tell us their names: Marcie and Rick. We proceed to tell them our story, and while we chat, Russell decides begging isn't against the rules. "Got any spare food? We could use something."

"Of course," Marcie says. "Cookies. Sunflower seeds . . ." My mouth waters. I think I even smile. Russell reaches out.

"No, thanks," I suddenly blurt out, coming to my senses. Like Blanche Dubois, I have always relied on the kindness of strangers, but I am determined to forsake all outside assistance. "We really can't accept a handout. If we were to happen upon some food somewhere, like some coconuts hanging from a tree, that'd be okay, but we can't come out and ask for food. Can we, Russell?"

Russell stares at me in disbelief, mouth agape. "Well, I guess that's that," he says.

Marcie and Rick wish us luck and head off. They're picnicking at our next campsite for lunch and say they'll check on us on the way back. A few hours pass, in which we only manage another mile. Marcie and Rick stop us in the middle of Lostman's Five Bay to rave about the campsite ahead of us. "You don't want to miss it!" Marcie yells and then they're gone. I look around at Russell's nightmare—the ever-present mangroves, a solitary royal palm, and the muddled water beneath us—and wonder what could be so special about this campsite. We explain away their enthusiasm as super-upbeat-Californiaism (Rick's from San Francisco).

Russell takes a stroke, retrieves his paddle, and rests it across the plastic gunwale. I rudder on the same side. Seconds flit by. Russell slowly drags his paddle through the water, then rests upon the gunwale again. I rudder some more. This we repeat for an hour. Occasionally I throw in a bona fide j-stroke on the opposite side. Russell talks seriously about turning around. I'm sad the Everglades has kicked our collective ass so quickly. We approach the mound. A hundred yards or so from the mound, I spy a garbage bag hanging from a tree. "Aw, man, what kind of fucking idiot would do that out here?" I complain.

Russell scrambles ashore with great speed and agility and grabs the bag off the mangrove branches. Rick and Marcie have given us their leftovers: a box of Entenmann's chocolate chip cookies, a half-bag of sunflower seeds, some pretzels, and nearly a loaf of sliced sourdough bread. We spread the riches across a park picnic table.

"We probably shouldn't eat it, huh? " Russell asks, not looking me in the eye.

"No," I answer, ripping into the cookies. "We should definitely eat it now," I improvise. "It's okay for someone to leave us something to find—we just can't ask for it and have it handed over to us. That's the rule. Understand?"

Day 5. Broad River. Russell catches a ten-pound grouper in the afternoon in a narrow canal called a cut-off between the Rodgers and Broad rivers. Salvation followed by salvation. However, we don't reach the campsite at the mouth of Broad River, dragging our dying fish beside the boat, until nine that night, thanks to a storm-driven ebb tide that forces the

water against us, six hours past the tide's scheduled turn. The campsite sits on a sandy hill just around the corner from the Gulf of Mexico—a perfect spot for the tornado that will fly over our tent a few hours later. A boatload of rednecks with six coffin-length coolers, a generator, and a radio playing "Raindrops Keep Falling on My Head" have taken the best spot. I smell fried chicken. They're swilling Bud in perspiring cans. They offer us nothing.

Twenty minutes after our arrival, the fish, reduced to roughly two 1½-pound fillets, rests in our stomachs. It feels like we haven't eaten a thing.

Day 6. The Gulf of Mexico. "Thank God, we're outta that alligator muck," Russell exults. "We can finally take a swim in peace." Moments later a passing shark, more than half the length of our canoe, nearly swamps us as I'm still thinking about his words. I've read on the park's Web site that the best thing to do when encountering an alligator while swimming is to appear as large as possible so the alligator will be intimidated. I haven't seen any information regarding swimming with sharks, so we opt to keep paddling.

We've decided to skip our original route, heading more directly for Flamingo by not taking the winding shallow path through Broad Creek. With any luck, tonight we'll stay at Graveyard Creek campsite at the mouth of Ponce de Leon Bay. We're not registered to use the site, but it's a beach. There's gotta be enough room.

Contrary to popular lore, Ponce de León was searching for riches, not a fountain of youth when he discovered and named Florida in 1513. His goal was to make his name by exhausting the plenitude that Florida offered, and he was damned good at it. One night he and his gang of Spanish conquerors slaughtered 160 tortoises, 14 seals, and 5,000 birds. After exploring the Florida coast and killing some unruly Calusa, he returned to Cuba, daunted but not defeated. In 1521 he went back to Florida bent on domination. One hot afternoon, not too far north of the bay, while he was trying to figure out the best way to pluck slaves out of the wilds of the Everglades, a Calusa arrow interrupted his musings. Marjory Stoneman Douglas, defender of the Everglades, took great delight in capturing this scene in her defining work, *The Everglades: River of Grass:* ". . . there came that curious twang of a released bowstring, and in the next instant the *thlock* [my italics] of an arrow reaching its mark. They stared at a man spinning and clutching at his throat, with an arrow sticking through it, stared as he fell and flopped like a fish. . . . Ponce de León himself, the conquistador, the great general, rallied his men around him, his eyes flashing with the old light. There must have been a great sense of conquest surging up in the men about him, a great shouting and cheering as the adelantado strode up the sand, his sword drawing light. An arrow hissed and struck deep in a joint in his armor. So Ponce de León bled, and his blood is the same scarlet as the blood of all of them spilled on that trampled whiteness underfoot. That is all he is ever to give Florida, besides her discovery and her name. She gave him his death for it."

At Graveyard Creek (aptly named, at least in our minds), a beachfront campsite cooled by a nearly constant south wind, we finally break park rules and forage. We spot two dried-up coconuts in a palm tree and spend an hour getting them down. Later, I catch two crabs and one very bony fish slightly larger than my hand. We eat well before sundown but feel no real sustenance.

I begin to like the weak feeling that's blanketing my body—it's a perfect opiate. I finally understand why dictators get away with so much. When you're really depleted, you really don't care as all you want to do is lie down and take it easy. In this state I am sure we have entered the very soul of our outing, that by starving, we have put our finger on the pulse of the Everglades, and it beats a simple truth, this pulse: Go away, go away, go away. . . .

This part of the Everglades, and perhaps the entire ecosystem, is wholly inhospitable. That's why Watson was killed in the Everglades; the place drives white men crazy. It's really no use to us and it's scary. That's why the State of Florida, perhaps America's most successful devourer of nature, has allowed the existence of this national park.

Yes, more-accomplished foragers than ourselves could have scrounged up a few snacks, and better fishermen might have had more luck, but on a subsistence level, on a welcoming level, the Everglades sucks. It's a lovely mangrove estuary when viewed from a fan boat or seen in a magazine while munching on a hearty slice of key lime pie, but taken at its most basic level, mano-a-eco, it's a hellhole.

Day 7. Some chickee. Edge of Whitewater Bay. My mind is a blank. Something monstrous takes Russell's baited hook and swims away with all: his bait, line, pole, and reel. We hear the pole crash to the deck of the chickee, watch it bounce across the pressure treated boards, and disappear into the murky shallows surrounding us. All we can do is watch. It's our second pole lost to the Everglades but we can't do a thing about it. Russell bought the pole with his American Express card and wonders aloud if they'll believe this story and reimburse him.

Day 8. Florida Bay. Ditto on the blank mind. Oh, and we make it to Flamingo, a threadbare outpost of a few cinderblock buildings, a marina, and park service apartments built on stilts. It's populated by transients, park employees, and crazies who were chased out of Key West by that town's comparative gentrification. Florida Bay stretches out beyond the seawall, its mangrove islands beckoning in that shimmering heat that makes you just want to swoon, if you're a nineteenth-century corset-wearing lady, that is. Personally, I sit down and eat a Snickers.

Squeezing Periphyton

IT WAS TIME FOR FURTHER HELP IN MY ATTEMPT TO UNDER-stand the Everglades, so I turned to the people at Everglades National Park. They suggested I take a hike—in those flat saw grass prairies you drive by on your way to somewhere else in South Florida.

Steve Robinson, an itinerant Everglades National Park naturalist, who looks like a card-carrying member of ZZ Top, would be my guide. His long ponytail and graying beard lend him a sage-like quality, a Moses amongst the saw grass—only this prophet doesn't want to part the waters; he wants to *un*part them.

Steve starts talking, teaching, preaching, the second we meet at Pahayokee Overlook in the middle of the park. *Pahayokee*, meaning "grassy waters," is the Seminole word for the Everglades, and if you've ever been down there, you know how apt a name it is. We've walked across a board-walk to a wooden platform, the kind the U.S. Park Service loves to build all over the country, and are gazing across an endless landscape of tall grass decorated, here and there, with an island of trees.

"This was Marjory Stoneman Douglas's favorite place in the park. She'd drive up here in her car, sit back, and watch her baby," Steve says, using an intimate tone. "She was a great woman, but the funny thing about her is that she didn't actually like going into the Everglades—all the mos-quitoes and dangers didn't interest her personally. She pre-ferred watching it from afar." He's got to be joking. The Mother Teresa of the Everglades didn't actually like entering the Everglades? All those quotes used to rally support around saving the Everglades—"There's no other place like it in the world" and "River of Grass,"—and she didn't even really like being in the place?

In 1947 Rinehart and Company published Douglas's *The Everglades: River of Grass* as part of its Rivers of America series, a year before the Interior Department made the lower Everglades a national park. The publisher had wanted Douglas to write about the Saint Johns River, but Douglas, a reporter for her father's *Miami Herald*, had written about the Everglades for the paper in the 1920s and '30s and was a member of the early committees to turn the Everglades into a national park. Douglas wanted to write about a subject closer to her heart, something a bit more controversial than the Saint Johns. The result was a four-hundred-page dense tome that covered everything from Florida's geological beginnings to Indian affairs, as well as every conceivable subject con-cerning the Everglades. Contemporaneous reviews of Douglas's book were complimentary, but it was not a big seller. Even so, it eventually became every fledgling Florida environmentalist's bible, and to this day, it sells about 10,000 copies a year. She died in 1998 at the astonishing age of 108.

Douglas won a number of O. Henry Awards for her short stories, and her book is one of the most lyrical works about history and nature that I've ever attempted to read. I say attempted, because I've never been able to read the whole thing from cover to cover, although she creates poetic images that build on themselves until you find yourself swept into the river's gentle flow. Douglas on Everglades' dew: "In the winter dry season, there takes place here another and gentler phenomenon of the equatorial tropics. In a windless dawn, in some light winter ground fogs, in mists that stand over the Everglades watercourses, the dew creeps like heavy rain down the shining heavy leaves, drips from the sawgrass edges, and stands among the coarse blossoming sedges and the tall ferns. Under the tree branches it is a steady soft Drop, drop and drip, all night long. In the first sunlight the dew, a miracle of freshness, stands on every leaf and wall and petal, in the finest of tiny patterns, in bold patterns of wide-strung cobwebs; like pearls in a silvery melting frostwork. . . ."

Rhythmic, to say the least. Her words bound along like this, sentence after sentence, paragraph after paragraph, for four hundred pages. You admire these words; delight in their fancy; even find yourself longing to be in the Everglades, but also, more often than not, you drop the book, sound asleep from sheer exhaustion. Human minds weren't made for such escalating grandeur. So I always find it funny when I see environmental groups, the park service, even sugar companies in their public relations material quoting from *River of Grass*. How many of these people have read this book? Better yet, how many of you have read it in its entirety? Two or three, a dozen?

51

Even so, *River of Grass* is the bible and Douglas is the prophet and I find myself chuckling at the thought that this woman, who could delight in the tiniest dewdrop within the Everglades, didn't really like the place. It causes me to like her and the book a little bit more and draws me in a step closer. Nothing like irony to make my heart grow fonder.

Breaking from this reverie, Steve and I step right into the dreaded saw grass after a short car ride down the park road that bisects the lower southeastern quadrant of the park. Yes, we're wading right into the saw grass. Stories abound of the grass ripping hapless explorers to shreds. This stuff is supposed to be evil incarnate—the other side of Eden, one touch and you're bleeding. Everybody knows this, if they know anything about the Everglades. Steve grabs a stalk of saw grass and firmly pulls upward, allowing the stalk to slip through his hand. So much for my finding an expert—he's a total loon (or more pertinent to the locale, a reddish egret—nature's Lucille Ball).

I look around for something to wipe the blood up with, but of course, he's not bleeding. It's only when you go against it—like fall down onto it (something I will do a lot of later)—that saw grass slices your skin like butter. "Sedges have edges. Rushes are round, and grass grows up from the ground," goes an old school rhyme. The edges of saw grass are razor sharp but only on the almost-microscopic upper inside edge.

If you've memorized the above rhyme, you realize saw grass is a sedge, not a grass. It's an emergent species that does all its business aboveground. That's why it has to be so tough and strong or it never would have survived for all these thousands of years. Yet playing with saw grass, as instructed, tickles.

Next, we squeeze periphyton—a spongy, Dijon-mustard-colored city of algae and microscopic creatures that floats on the surface and covers nearly everything growing beneath. Periphyton cleanses the Everglades of excess nutrients and pollutants. The chemical equation is pretty simple: Saw grass likes fairly neutral water and periphyton neutralizes acidic water. Without periphyton, the saw grass prairie is overrun by invasive vegetation like cattails (which has conquered places like the Loxahatchee National Wildlife Refuge on account of farm runoff), the river's flow is interrupted, and the slimy green algae, which doesn't nurture fish the way the periphyton does, takes over. The numbers of fish diminish. So do birds. The Everglades, as a whole, withers.

Things don't seem so bad to me here, though. There's plenty of periphyton. The air smells sweet, playing its way in fits and starts through the saw grass, which sways like a sea of western prairie. The water is clear, nothing like the murk over in the waterway. This is surprising for something that is often referred to as America's biggest swamp, but then here, in the park, it isn't a swamp. It's still a shallow, laid-back river, flowing imperceptibly southwest for forty or so miles.

Steve is frowning, repeatedly dipping his net into the water and coming up empty. He has brought the net along to show me the tiny fish that thrive in the saw grass and sporadic cypress stands.

"We should be seeing hundreds of fish, countless mosquito fish the size of my pinky. In past good years I could swoop my net through the water just as I'm doing now and come up with dozens at a time," he says, pulling up another empty net.

I offer it might just be a bad day.

"Maybe," he answers, but looks at me as if I just don't get it.

By this point we've waded under a graying dome of cypress, and we're standing in chest-high water. All in all, I'm feeling pretty casual. I've stopped jerking my head around every few seconds. My mind isn't racing with intricate escape plans, and I'm peering into the depths without worrying about being attacked from behind. Then I remember the snakes. The Everglades has twenty-six species of snakes and four types are poisonous: the eastern diamondback rattlesnake (*Crotalus adamanteus*), the coral snake (*Micrurus fulvius*), the pigmy rattlesnake (*Sistrurus miliarius*), and the water moccasin or cottonmouth (*Agkistrodon piscivorus*). They can all deliver their venom while swimming.

The coral snake has two impersonators: the scarlet and scarlet king snakes. They're not poisonous, but they like the same hideouts—places like our present location. All three of these snakes have red, yellow, and black stripes, but you're supposed to be able to tell the difference between them by the fact that the coral snake has a black snout and the other two have a red snout. Also, the two harmless snakes' red and yellow rings are separated by the black while the coral snake's red and yellow rings touch. That last bit has struck me as a tad dubious. I can just imagine frantically splashing backward, pissing in my pants (which in this high, warm water won't be noticed), and suddenly realizing, "Oh, that's a scarlet snake. Silly me. The separated colored rings give it away." It isn't going to happen.

I express my concerns to Steve.

"Yeah, there are a few poisonous species," Steve says in response to my quavering query. "Used to be, I'd see one or two every time I came out here. But again, there's another indicator that things aren't working: I haven't seen a single one in the past ten years. Things are bad and they're not going to get better anytime soon."

He really wants to show me the fish, so we keep wading and talking. "The organisms that sustain the Everglades are tiny, and we just don't focus on that. People see alligators in the park and think everything is good. That's ridiculous. Alligators are not a biological indicator of a healthy system by any means. You can create a golf course out of this and you'd still have your alligators." Even so, we're in perfect alligator territory, the deep pools flooding the cypresses, but they're not here. They're clustered closer to Shark River Slough, a few miles through the saw grass north of here. Steve says the alligators know there'll be water there year-round, as opposed to where we are. This place'll be as dry as a Baptist revival by March. All this water, gone. The few fish we see, dead.

Steve points out different grasses and sedges and plants. I particularly like the bladderworts, floating plants that look like their name, that catch bugs in their baglike mouths. The tall cypress above us, hundreds of years old, are connected by orbed-spider nests and hanging plants. I ask him about the smaller cypress that you see when driving down the park road. They've lost their leaves and look dead. What's killed them? I wonder.

"Visitors to the park always ask that. They're not dead. Those little trees simply lost their leaves over the winter. Most of those small ones [about twelve feet high with trunks the size of fence posts] are more than a hundred years old. They can live here and be somewhat successful, even with the Everglades as it is, but they're on a strict diet—like paddling the Everglades Waterway without food," he says, a friendly little jab. When his net continues to come up empty, he suggests we walk back to a culvert on the other side of the road. It's the best place in the park to watch fish and invertebrate life.

We stretch out alongside the concrete culvert. The water flows surprisingly swiftly, but then again, it's such a small place for all that water to drain through—a million acres of water draining through a dozen or so culverts along the park road—that you'd think it would be flowing even faster. We watch finger-length fish feed on bugs and smaller fish. Crawfish creep out of their underwater dungeons. Water bugs skitter by.

Steve keeps talking. I imagine he can talk about the Everglades all day long, all night, and even into the next morning until he passes out from exhaustion. He speaks about the water level the way some parents do about their baby's growth chart. It's all-encompassing, a matter of life or death—not just for the animals that should live here but also for him. When he's away in the summer, working at Oregon's Crater Lake, colleagues in Florida keep him updated on a regular basis.

"People don't think the park will ever be what it once was, but these people aren't from Florida. They've never seen what it was like here. I've grown up here; I'm a third generation Floridian. I have this vision of original Florida that my grandpa showed me, etched in my memory.

"I've noticed that after every drought period we've had since I've been working at the park—twenty-five years— that the comeback never reaches the level it is before. It has never truly come back. Sure, it'd be better once the rains came, then it'd take it on the chin in the dry season. Then the next rainy season, it'd come back to an even lower level. That's why I can't get very excited about this latest solution, the so-called Everglades Restoration Plan, because it's a 10-percent solution at best."

The Everglades Lorax has spoken.

* * *

The next day I go snorkeling at the federal- and state-protected reef southeast of Key Largo—an area seemingly far removed from the worries and troubles of the Everglades. A tour boat drops fifty of us off about a mile off-shore, giving us two hours to explore the reef. The mate, almost as an afterthought, admonishes us not to step on the reef because this will damage or kill the coral—a laughable suggestion considering what we were about to see. Being a swimmer, I cover a wide area, perhaps more than a mile, in the given time. I see a tragedy—not in the making but an already full-blown tragedy. The mate failed to mention anything about the reef mostly being dead, but healthy coral usually makes you feel like you're in a psychedelic, drug-inspired Hunter Thompson adventure. This is more like a step into *Apocalypse Now*. The coral is colorless, scarred, and truncated. There are no urchins feeding on algae, a typical reef scene, and the few remaining fish zip by fruitlessly searching for food.

Mainland America's largest living coral reef is fast becoming America's largest dead coral reef. Man, this is going to make a funny story. Me and the tourists together, staring death straight in the face and not even knowing it.

I go back home to Maine to write my sarcastic bit about these "so obvious" ironies. Then, one day, sitting at my computer, I remember that moment when the Everglades seemed different: The wind had bent the saw grass in visible trails, as if ghosts were playing a game of tag; I didn't see any roads or hear any planes, and all I could smell was the warm sweetness of the saw grass. It was the epitome of peace.

So, now, I suddenly want that moment again, and I decide to look into the Everglades a bit more. This river may or may not be on the verge of hearing its last rites, but it has drawn me further in, against my initial instinct.

A Rich Mead of Praise

IT'S BEEN FOUR YEARS SINCE I WAS DRAWN FURTHER IN, AND on the surface much has happened. On July 1, 1999, Vice President Al Gore, Captain Planet, presented the U.S. Army Corps of Engineers plan to restore the Everglades to Congress, boldly going where no vice president had gone before: "Saving the Everglades is a national priority. . . . Never before have we worked on such a grand scale to restore our environment."

On December 11, 2000, surrounded by congressmen, Florida's Governor Jeb Bush, sugar growers, and environmentalists, President Bill Clinton bit his lower lip and with glistening eyes signed the Comprehensive Everglades Restoration Plan into law. His office informed the world, "The Comprehensive Everglades Restoration Plan will return a natural flow of water through the Everglades. . . . President Clinton and Vice President Gore have made the restoration of the Florida Everglades a major environmental priority."

Then, on January 10, 2002, President Bush signed an agreement with Florida's governor, his brother Jeb, dealing with South Florida water usage. The agreement guaranteed water captured with new technology being developed under the plan "will not be permitted for a consumptive use or otherwise made available by the State of Florida until such time as sufficient reservations of water for the restoration of the natural system are made. . . ." Confusing, yes, but President Bush topped off the intentionally vague jargon with a declaration similar to Gore's and Clinton's: "The Everglades and the entire South Florida ecosystem are a unique national treasure. The restoration of this ecosystem is a priority for my Administration, as well as for Governor Bush."

South Florida a national treasure? Many of us have been there, but I think few of us in our heart of hearts thinks of its ecosystem as a national treasure. It's our winter escape—a place that many claim is godawful, tacky, and overdeveloped while returning again and again. When we're there, we bodysurf in the ocean, swim in a motel pool, eat some local fish, watch a dolphin frolic in the waves, and maybe even spot an endangered manatee feeding in the shallows. And, without a doubt, we all take a sip of water.

Yet, sure enough, all of this comes courtesy of the Everglades. It's fed the fish, filled the pools, sustained the mammals since the beginning, and it was, is, and forever shall be the primary source of South Florida's drinking water, which is truly remarkable, considering all that has been done to this fragile treasure. The classic Everglades, the one everyone is trying to save or restore or whatever is claimed, only existed for some five thousand years before we started diking, draining, and leveeing it apart.

What did it look like in the beginning? Here's the standard answer: It was like no other river in the world; it flowed at $\frac{1}{48}$ mph for 100 miles from Lake Okeechobee's shallow waters down to Florida Bay and the Gulf of Mexico, its banks up to seventy miles apart, its average depth measured in inches, not feet.

Scientists have figured out a few other things. The Florida Plateau, essentially the plate of earth that Florida and much of its surrounding waters sit on, was originally a part of what became the African continent, near Senegal. (Scientists believe this because the plateau's basement rock—the bottom of the bottom—is the same as the basement rock in West Africa.) In those early years the Florida Plateau was passed around like some unwanted child in a failed marriage, as the continents got together and broke up several times, all the while lying calmly beneath a shallow sea. Plants and animals died in its waters, sank to the bottom, and their decomposition in the saltwater created calcium carbonate, better known as limestone. Layer piled upon layer, creating a foundation of death for the future Everglades to inhabit. Even when that giant meteor hit the nearby Yucatán peninsula, wiping out all the dinosaurs, the limestone just kept on slowly rising. The Florida Plateau wasn't shaken up and stayed decidely flat, except for a slight southwestwardly tilt (the all-important tilt that led directly to the Everglades' creation).

Finally, around 25 million years B.C., land poked out of the ocean for the very first time below Georgia. The Sunshine State had arrived.

The area that would become Lake Okeechobee and the Everglades remained underwater, however, gathering ever more limestone—all told, thirteen thousand feet of it accumulated near the lake and twenty thousand down near Florida Bay. These massive deposits never rose above sea level, though, because the bottom of the plateau sank at a nearly equal rate—a result, we're told, of plate tectonics. Then the various ice ages began wreaking their havoc. When the water levels dropped because so much of the Earth's waters were frozen, more of the plateau rose above sea level, only to disappear again as the ice melted, a period called Flandrian Transgression.

The land created in present-day Florida during the ice ages was a dry, parched desert, where mighty winds swept sand dunes from one place to another. It was so dry because saltwater is heavier than fresh; so when the oceans receded there was nothing left to hold in rainwater. It just trickled away. During some of the ice ages, Florida was much bigger than today and in others, it was smaller, depending on how much of the Earth's water was turned to ice. (In the Wisconsin ice age, the last one so far, as the woolly mammoths were frozen, the oceans drew back again and Florida was more than twice as large as today, a developer's dream.)

When the Wisconsin ice age came to an end, mountains of ice broke off of glaciers, rivers swelled to the size of seas, and oceans rose, much like what might happen in the not-too-distant future if the most drastic predictions concerning global warming continue to come true. Humans scurried back to the trees and Florida, shorter in stature, was swallowed-up to its current size.

The ferocious winds that had swept sand dunes across Florida died down and mounds came to a rest on both sides of the peninsula, adding to two confining formations that had grown during all the other Flandrian Transgressions: one not too far inland on South Florida's east coast, and a similar one on the west coast, Florida's only natural levees.

Between the twenty-five-foot-high ridge on the East Coast and forty-two-foot-tall one on the West Coast, the ocean was shallow, not more than a few feet deep, but there it was, for thousands of years afterward.

Although under saltwater, the Everglades was becoming a confined space, as old sand dunes hardened into place. At this point, some ten thousand years ago, the heavier saltwater would push the fresh water to the surface of the old limestone that was now above sea level. This occurred mostly around the Kissimmee River Basin (Disney World on down to Lake Okeechobee). Wetland plants, like arrowhead, willow, cattail, and saw grass, blossomed for the first time. Those wetlands, and their evolving flora and fauna, slowly drained southwesterly, and they ever-so-slowly began to crowd out the shallow saltwater. Over thousands of years Lake Okeechobee started to take shape. The wetlands didn't stop there, though. They crept farther and farther southward, because of peculiarities in the limestone, the old southwest slant of the Florida Plateau bedrock, and crucial dry periods, the last of which allowed fires to enrich the soil by killing plants and animals—the decaying organic matter creating an even richer soil for the next wave of flora. Over time, these cyclical wet and dry periods created peat and muck as new plants emerged from the dead and then died back themselves.

Nearly seven eons passed in this manner. Elsewhere, the Egyptians built some mastabas, and as if erecting those tapering monstrosities weren't enough, some genius created a need for an even higher, slave-killing structure: the pyramid. The Polynesians were navigating the Pacific seas by the sway of their testicles. The Greeks weren't yet philosophizing, but King Minos was sitting on the first wooden toilet seat. Meanwhile, back in North America, the encroaching wetlands had finally reached the frontline: Florida Bay. Around 3000 B.C. the Everglades emerged full born.

By this point Homo sapiens had been inhabiting the eastern and western ridges of South Florida for thousands of years. Were these early inhabitants anxiously watching the arrival of saw grass and periphyton in their neighborhood? Highly doubtful. It's anybody's guess, but judging from various middens—garbage heaps, really—we do know that as the Everglades dominated the interior and people adapted to coastal life, nearly 90 percent of their diet came to consist of things that swim.

As can be seen from the dry data collected from the various living sites on the coastal ridges of the Everglades, humans increasingly occupied this new ecosystem, adapting to its lifestyle with each successive generation. Having no metal or even hard stones, they fashioned weapons and tools from bones and shells. They also used the shells from mollusks and bivalves to create new dry land, same as lower Manhattan or Boston's Back Bay was created. In fact, much of the land in what is now the western edge of the Everglades National Park was made from shell landfill. Florida's first archeologists labeled these early people the Shellfish Eaters, although current scientists believe shellfish played only a minor role in their overall diet. Equally minor but still present in their diet were edible wild plants, from coco plums to the shoots of red mangroves to maize. Apparently, the early inhabitants cultivated nothing, but then again, why bother? The whole place was one big smorgasbord of shellfish, fruit, and fish.

As with so many other early preliterate people, we don't know much more about the early Floridians than their diet, although archeologists have found tool fragments, bones, ceramics wares, and shreds of clothing from virtually every century since the last ice age. We know their eating habits and artisan skills so we know what they ate and how they ate it. But we don't know how they felt or what they thought of the Everglades as it burned, flooded, and dried its way into existence, through an ever-repeating cycle of creation.

Imagine sitting on one of those sand ridges looking down at a patch of muck, resting from an "all you can eat" fish feast. The muck doesn't look all that appealing, so you spit and walk back to the beach. The next year, when your people have migrated back to the fishing grounds near Marco Island, thin stalks of saw grass have risen a foot out of the water, which is clearer than before. Next time you come back—well, maybe that year you can't come back. The whole world seems to be on fire. The smoke and heat keep you and your clan farther north. The fires come on so fast you even forget your favorite club made from the skull of a hammerhead shark. Ah, but you return the next year, only this time the stalks aren't as high, but there are millions more of them.

It's not until English-speaking travelers happen on the scene that we get a detailed description of the Everglades. Ponce de León and his fellow conquerors start visiting Florida in the 1500s, as mentioned earlier, but these conquistadors were not really interested in ecosystems or descriptive geography. They were interested in riches, slaves, and converting souls to Christianity. They didn't spend much time describing their surroundings. A place was just a means to an end to them. And, as it turned out, there was no gold in the Everglades, not many souls to convert except along the coast, apparently no place to grow sugarcane (the crop that funded their American exploits elsewhere), and the Calusa and the Tequesta didn't take to being enslaved. Consequently, the

Spaniards didn't spend much time in the Everglades or even South Florida.

To catch a glimpse of the Everglades in those early days of European influence, we have suspect priests' accounts of human sacrifices conducted by the Calusa to ensure the safe return of the mullet or equally suspect castaway accounts. No fully reliable description of the Everglades is provided until traveling naturalists arrived on the scene two centuries later.

In the late 1700s Bernard Romans, a naturalist/surveyor, soldier/artist, botanist/writer based in Hartford, Connecticut, explored Florida and made one of its first usable full-scale maps. Romans, more intrepid than most, paddled and hiked more than twenty-four miles up the Saint Lucia River (today's Saint Lucie Canal—the Corps of Engineers' maintained waterway that allows boats to enter Lake Okeechobee from the Atlantic) until it opened up into a vast plain where the river lost its steep banks and was fringed only by trees. "Here we shot what number of deer, and turkies we pleased, and might have continued so to do, I dare say, two months longer." He was told by a fisherman, who'd been held captive by some Indians, that the Saint Lucia began at Lake Mayaca (Lake Okeechobee) and that the lake had five or six mouths either originating from or feeding into it. Romans correctly deduced from the volume of the Saint Lucia that Lake Mayaca was the source for so many of the rivers that poured into the Gulf and the Atlantic. His summations concerning the swamps, airs, and meadows of southern East Florida (from 1763 to 1783, Florida was in British hands and was divided into East and West Florida; East Florida encompassed much of present-day Florida, except for the panhandle; West Florida ran from Pensacola on over to the Mississippi River and up to Jackson, Mississippi) were especially evocative: "I will however venture to foretell, that on opening the woods of this country for cultivation, which will naturally drain ponds, gullies, and company, the air will be here very little affected by those pernicious vapors, which have so uncommon an influence over the humorous and fibrous parts of the human frame, as to destroy their harmonious concordance . . . and occasioning them to relax and thereby produce weaknesses, lassisitudes, and finally dangerous and fatal disorders." Although he's evidently a proponent of draining things, Romans advises against comprehensive drainage because "on draining them completely, they prove to be as arrant a sand as any in this country."

From Romans until the 1820s (when Florida was again in Spanish hands) we get few accounts of Florida's interior, most of which are about its impenetrable nature, the wealth of its land if only there was not so much water, and the hostile natives.

Then during the time Florida became a U.S. territory in 1821, a civil and topographical engineer named Charles Vignoles traveled throughout the peninsula and published the most extensive and well-surveyed map of Florida to that period. Vignoles was also the first person to publish the term *Ever Glades* to describe the interior waterlands in a book called *Observations Upon the Floridas* (published 1823). Marjory Stoneman Douglas and others have attributed first usage to the mapmaker Tanner, but Tanner, the publisher of Vignoles's map, simply copied Vignoles's work. I believe Vignoles was the first to print the term; perhaps he even coined it. According to Vignoles, "The Glade, or as it is emphatically termed the Never Glade, appears to occupy almost the whole interior from about the parallel of Jupiter Inlet to Cape Florida . . . with from six inches to two feet of water lying upon it, in which is a growth of saw, and other water grasses, so thick as to impede the passage of boats where there is no current." The name "Ever Glade" appears to evolve as Vignoles's book proceeds. He first calls it the Great Glade, then it's the Never Glade, and then again, about five pages later, he terms it the "Ever Glades." This is what he put on his map, written in capital letters closely spaced so that from then on, it appeared on other subsequent maps as the Everglades.

Vignoles was repulsed in his own attempts to enter the deepest parts of the Ever Glades, and for many years afterward white people stayed clear of the interior, except for the occasional hunter and trapper, until the Americans decided they had to get rid of the Seminole once and for all.

The Seminole, whose name means "separatists," broke off from the Creeks in the 1700s and moved into northern Florida the latter part of that century, absorbing the Apalachee tribe as they went along. However, even before Spain turned Florida over to the United States, American settlers wanted the Indians out of northern Florida and began attacking them, although apparently unprovoked. The Seminole struck back, attacking farms in southern Georgia. Andrew Jackson led the First Seminole War in 1817, effectively moving the Seminole farther south—into the Everglades and the surrounding coastal areas. The Second Seminole War, 1835–1842, erupted because the Americans had moved farther south as well, and were trying to force the Seminole to leave Florida for reservations in Oklahoma. The Seminole did not want to be evicted. Early guerrilla campaigners, they came in from the tall grass, attacked swiftly, and then disappeared back into the Everglades.

Retaliating, Americans penetrated the Everglades in great numbers for the first time. (Running at an estimated twenty million dollars, the Second Seminole War was the costliest Indian war ever and also the least successful. The Seminole were never completely forced out.) Following the Seminole example, the soldiers traversed the Everglades by canoe, lived off the land, and practiced Indian-style warfare. As a result, many white people saw the land's potential close-up. An anonymously penned account published in *The St. Augustine News* on January 8, 1841, laboriously details some skirmishes between the army and the Seminole from the previous month; while generally focused on the minutiae of battle, the author takes time to remark, "No country that I have ever heard of bears any resemblance to it; it seems like a vast sea, filled with grass and green trees, and expressly intended as a retreat for the rascally Indians . . . we gained dry land; here we found a corn field of about an acre, and the richest land I have ever seen, being one black heap of soil of endless depth."

Thanks to such accounts people seriously began to consider draining the Everglades for settlement and cultivation. According to the journal of a retired Rear Admiral George Henry Prebe, a dredge boat was working the New River, an outlet of the Everglades located near Fort Lauderdale, as early as 1842.

Just months after being granted statehood in 1845, the Florida legislature passed a resolution asking the U.S. government's aid in draining and dredging the Everglades, claiming "that at a comparatively small expense the afore-said region can be entirely reclaimed, thus opening to habitation of man an immense and hitherto unexplored domain perhaps not surpassed in fertility and every natural advantage by any other on the globe." Their rallying cry "Drain the swamp!" could be heard all the way up in Washington, D.C., where with a full-court press, the state's newly elected senator, J. D. Wescott, hounded the Secretary of the Treasury to authorize a study and survey with this end in mind. The question for Wescott and his fellow Floridians was never "if" but only "when."

American engineers, politicians, capitalists, and crackpots alike saw millions of subtropical acres wasted on useless plants, birds, and animals. This is how they thought: *Much of these acres are obviously submerged year-round, but a few million are dry, with more drying out temporarily each winter. Look at what they're growing on those temporarily dry areas already: sugarcane and succulent tropical fruits, like oranges, limes, and bananas, things that have to be imported from the Brits, the Dutch, the Spanish, and the French. If we could just hold that festering swampy water off a million or so more acres year-round, then the riches amassed for both individuals and the country would be practically inconceivable.* Even Vignoles agrees: "Since the manuscript of this work was completed, the accounts from East Florida, respecting the sugar cane, have been uncommonly favorable. . . . It is a matter of infinite satisfaction that the certainty of sugar becoming the staple of Florida is already established."

Just the thought of all these riches made grown men grow as breathless as a thirteen-year-old boy back then with a copy of Ingres's *Odalisque with a Slave.* Senator Wescott seems to have convinced every respected or learned person he came across to address the Secretary of the Treasury regarding the Everglades' drainage. Generals, writers, politicians, engineers—all sent letters attesting to the Everglades' drainability—all without the existence of a single survey of the Everglades.

Eventually the Treasury Secretary responded to the badgering and authorized one Buckingham Smith to examine the land offices in Florida and procure "authentic information in relation to what are generally called the 'Everglades' on the peninsula of Florida." Every single book and article I've come across regarding this appointment has labeled Smith's task, and subsequent report, a survey, although the Secretary's letter to Smith indicates otherwise: "You are not expected to make a survey. . . ." But it was suggested that he, without instruments, "approximate to the relative elevation of the waters in the rivers of the Gulf and Atlantic coasts, opposite to the Everglades, with the waters in the Everglades; and you can ascertain pretty correctly the general depth of the water in the lake and the probable quantity of land that can be reclaimed by draining it by canals into those rivers."

Why had they asked this of Buckingham Smith? He wasn't an engineer and he'd never been in the Everglades. He was, however, a well-known and respected citizen of Florida, engaged in local government, small farming enterprises, the law, and writing. More to the point, he wanted to go to Mexico City and Madrid to translate the papers, documents, and manuscripts concerning the Spanish conquistadors in America. Being of limited funds—his government-employee father died when Buckingham was fifteen—he was ready to do anything to be sent there. His friends in Washington knew this because he pestered them endlessly to intercede on his behalf.

Smith questioned all the experts, mainly meaning the people Wescott had enlisted to petition Congress for drainage. He went to the land offices as required and actually made a short trip into the Everglades itself in a Navy boat.

Lo and behold, several months later he recommended drainage. In fact, he didn't just recommend drainage; he made it sound like a saintly duty—that whosoever began the venture would be considered the greatest of greats: "The citizen . . . who succeeds in making fit for cultivation, even if but partially, a region . . . now as useless as the deserts of Africa, will earn a rich mead of praise from the people of Florida and of the Union. The Everglades are now suitable only for the haunt of noxious vermin, or the resort of pestilent reptiles."

This man knew how to push every button imaginable on a politician: vanity, fear, greed, duty, intelligence, and compassion. "The statesman whose exertions shall cause the millions of acres they contain, now worse than worthless, to teem with the products of agricultural industry," Smith stated, ". . . will merit a high place in public favor, not only with his own generation, but with posterity. He will have created a State. . . ."

Smith didn't have the experience or knowledge of the soldiers and hunters who'd entered the Glades before him, but he did have the motivation and a way with words. Before reading Smith's report, I'd always imagined that the rush to drain the Everglades was simply a capitalistic impulse, driven by lust for money and power. For sure, that was what drove many of its proponents, but it's not what drove Smith. Smith needed access—the Everglades was simply a means to his end. So he artfully played on the theme that he knew would open the doors, not only for him, but also for his state. He made it our American duty to drain the Everglades. He moved the task from being a mere regional issue to a national cause—a platform for election for politicians from his day until now. It became something for "We the People," creating opportunity, opening the doors to fulfillment—whether this be monetary success or happiness or both.

And so Smith made the case for reclaiming the Everglades,

and he was rewarded amply. His friends produced the much-desired appointment to Mexico and then Spain. He served as secretary of the legations (representation slightly below an embassy) in Mexico and Spain in the 1850s and made his translations of the Conquistadors' feats, which are still used today by students and scholars.

Funny, that term: *reclaiming*. Weren't these early Floridians actually "claiming" the Everglades? Had it ever been theirs to re-claim? While reclaim comes from the Latin *reclamare*: to cry out, exclaim. In English, it came to mean both "to keep in check or restrain" and "to claim again." By the 1700s, when used in connection with land, it referred to drying out land that was covered in water.

To repeat a point, man was reclaiming land from the Flood—earnestly fulfilling the covenant God made with Noah, the one where he told Noah after the flood to "Be fruitful then and multiply, teem over the earth and subdue it!" In this context, and in the context of the pious Christians of mid-nineteenth-century America, reclaiming could be construed to be a religious obligation—taking back what God had first given and then taken from us so that we could continue to prosper and multiply.

The funny thing about Buckingham Smith, though, is that even while he was performing his American duty, he was clearly pulled in another direction. If you track down Smith's full report, something I could only do with the help of Florida International University's online Everglades librarian Megan Waters, another side to Mr. Buckingham Smith is revealed—a side that appears to reflect his heart and his own sensibilities, as opposed to the sensibilities of his day and even his unyielding need to ingratiate himself. For all his talk about "worse than worthless" and useless-ness, his most powerful descriptions of the Everglades itself bring to mind serenity, beauty, and a place of respite. Yes, he judged the Everglades worthless and damned it for all eternity, but he described it otherwise:

> The flexible grass bending gently to the breeze protects the waters from its influence. Lilies and other aquatic flowers of every variety and hue are to be seen on every side, in pleasant contrast with the pale green of the saw grass, and as you draw near an island the beauty of the scene is increased by the rich foliage and looming flowers of the wild myrtle and the honeysuckle and other shrubs and vines that generally adorn its shores. The profound and wild solitude of the place, the solemn silence that pervades it, unless broken by the splashing of a paddle of the canoe or light bateau, with which only can you traverse the Pahayokee, or by the voices of your "compagnons du voyage" add to awakened and excited curiosity, feelings bordering on awe.

Even when being condemned to its sapped future, the Everglades reached out to Smith and soothed him, and he was won over by its fragile beauty. Shortly after the preceding description, however, Smith slaps himself out of this reverie, adding: "The effect of such visit to the Pahayokee upon a person of romantic imagination and who indulges his fancies on such subjects, it may be presumed, would be somewhat poetic. But if the visitor is a man of practical utilitarian turn of thought, the first and the abiding impression is the utter worthlessness to civilized man, in its present condition, for any useful or practical object, of the entire region . . . in my judgment the experiment is worth a trial."

Others—soldiers, politicians, businessmen, do-gooders—had all petitioned presidents, the secretary of the treasury, Congress, their grandmothers to do something about the Everglades, but Smith's report finally opened the drain. With the report in hand, Senator Wescott introduced Senate Bill 338 of 1848, which gave all the land, watery or not, below, and including, Lake Okeechobee to the State of Florida with one major condition: "The said State shall, on or before the first day of January, eighteen hundred and fifty-one, cause to be commenced, under the direction of a competent engineer . . . the construction of drains and canals, to be sufficient, if practicable, for draining the Everglades aforesaid, and for reclaiming the subaqueous land thereof . . . and said State shall cause said works to be completed and finished within ten years. . . ."

The year 1851 rolled around, however, and not much had been dug. Buckingham Smith was in Mexico, head of the legation. Florida and the U.S. Army were conducting the Third Seminole War. And although it was estimated that it would cost only three hundred thousand to five hundred thousand dollars to pull the plug, that was a hell of a lot of money for Florida—one of the poorest states in the country—equal to a state coming up with $6 million to $10 million today.

Although Florida had been so gung ho for draining, nothing happened. Years drifted by, wars came and went, and the Everglades was mostly forgotten. By 1880 or so, Florida had gotten itself into a financial mess, mismanaging state land and funds, shady stuff that might even make the executives at Enron blush. Governor Bloxham of Florida decided the way out was through selling the land to anybody who would reclaim it. He quickly found such a person in Hamilton Disston, a tourist who had been coming down to Florida to fish lunker bass for the past decade.

Ham, as he liked to be called, was the son of a successful and wealthy saw manufacturer. Like nearly anybody whose father has money, he wanted to continue to live off it. But he was also a man of ideas, and boy did he like this one about draining the Everglades.

The contract between Disston and the state, signed on March 11, 1881, stipulated that if Disston and his associates would drain all overflowed land south of Township 24 (three miles north of Kissimmee) and east of Peace Creek, the group would receive alternate sections of all reclaimed land—potentially some 10 million acres. Afterward, though, the trustees of the board running the fund controlling these lands for the State of Florida refused to honor the contract because the fund was in receivership for $1 million. Disston would be getting a lot of land and the state would still be short its $1 million. However, the determined governor worked out a deal with Disston, who agreed to buy 4 million acres for the outstanding $1 million that the state owed.

The only hitch was that Ham didn't have $1 million or a dredge. So he repackaged the underwater land as viable real estate and sold off nearly 2 million acres so he could pay the state the $1 million he owed. Only then could he buy two dredges and have them shipped down to Florida.

The name of Disston's company, lest there be any mistaking his goal, was the Atlantic and Gulf Coast Canal and Okeechobee Land Company. The company planned to drain the upper Everglades by opening up east and west going canals from Lake Okeechobee—Okeechobee sits forty miles from the Atlantic and roughly eighty miles east of the Gulf. The western canal was begun immediately by digging out the preexisting Caloosahatchee, a clear meandering river with moss-laden trees dripping over its banks. It was quickly transmogrified into a silt-laden, runoff

ditch. However, most of Disston's efforts went into draining the Kissimmee River basin (headwaters for Lake
Okeechobee) with a gargantuan, Dr. Seuss–like digger to
create the land he'd already sold to finance all his activities. Coming down from the town of Kissimmee, the
dredger worked that area for close to three years. Disston
ended up with nearly 2 million acres, mostly west and
north of Lake Okeechobee, but his company, changing
names as frequently as Madonna does accents, was mis-
managed into the ground. The Great Financial Panic of
1893 ruined Ham and he "shot himself as he lay in his
bathtub," writes John Rothchild in *Up for Grabs*, "at least
ending his life with a successful drainage. . . ."

The eastern canal was never even attempted, and
although great claims were made about the ease and relative
cheapness of clearing the land and planting sugar cane, the
most Disston planted was one thousand acres. Lake
Okeechobee was not lowered significantly, but it was lowered; land around the Caloosahatchee dried out enough for
farmers and settlers to move in.

The Everglades could be drained.

Over the next two decades, the Florida legislature and
the overseers of the state's lands, the Internal Improvement
Fund board, newly debtless, just messed things up all over
again, giving away land to railroad companies that had no
intention of draining the Everglades. The federal government eventually got the land back for the state, but the state,
always desperate for cash, turned around and sold it to
more railroad companies. Then in 1905 Florida elected
Napoleon Bonaparte Broward governor. He tried to collect
taxes from the railroads, but they refused to pay. This time,
the Feds sided with the railroads, so Broward just created
new tax laws.

Meanwhile, Napoleon attacked the Everglades, having been elected on his promise to "drain that abominable, pestilence-ridden swamp." Brandishing a shady drainage report and questionable surveys, he began draining the Everglades by using nearly all of the Internal Improvement Funds money and selling even more land. He dynamited rapids, dug canals, and made draining the Everglades his sole reason for living, or at least for being elected. A much anticipated drainage report, commissioned by the federal government, claimed the Everglades could be thoroughly drained by digging eight canals. A million acres would be recovered. And it would only cost one dollar an acre to do so. The author of the report, a federal engineer named James O. Wright, had a history of corruption, having received kickbacks from land companies for surveys and reports he'd made in North Carolina while working there for the federal government. His Everglades report was a work of fiction, but it was all Florida needed.

After that, it was all over. Every desperate person in America wanted a piece of the Everglades. Hundreds of thousands of acres of the undrained Everglades were sold to dreamers and schemers alike for anything from a few dollars an acre to one hundred. Suddenly, thousands of people had a stake in Everglades drainage.

And, once again, things didn't happen like they were supposed to. The land wasn't drained; investors threw fits. Many sued. Others buckled down and worked the land anyway, only to find out that clearing the land at one dollar an acre was an impossibility.

Even so, the duped investors, along with new developers, railroad barons, and politicians, added their voices to the state's age-old battle cry, "Drain the Swamp!" and by 1926, things looked pretty good, at least for some of the farmers and hired hands living below Lake Okeechobee. Despite all the difficulties surrounding clearing the land, they had thousands of acres under the plow. In addition, the state and local communities had built an eight-foot dike that stretched across the southern perimeter of the lake to prevent flooding in times of heavy rain; trucks were leaving the area every week laden with tomatoes, vegetables, and fruits headed for the North.

With the dike, residents of fledgling lakeside communities like Moore Haven thought they were relatively safe, even though the dike gave way to the lake in 1924, causing minimal damage. Then, in the fall of 1926, another hurricane raged across the state, churning up Lake Okeechobee's shallow waters. The dike crumbled like a sand castle wall before the ocean's swells. Three hundred Moore Haven residents died, and floods covered millions of acres.

The Army Corps of Engineers, directed by Congress, studied the situation and concluded that they didn't need to do anything, except work on improving navigation from the Atlantic Ocean to the Gulf of Mexico through Lake Okeechobee. Then, another hurricane hit Florida in 1928 and it was even worse than the last one. Lake Okeechobee burst through its shabby confines once again. This time 2,400 people died and an estimated $59 million in property damage occurred. It remains the third-worst natural calamity in American history (behind Galveston's 1900 hurricane floods killing roughly eight thousand and San Francisco's 1906 earthquake taking three thousand lives).

The Corps studied the situation again and this time decided it should build a new dike and improve drainage. The U.S. government asked the state of Florida to pay for some 60 percent of the effort, but by this time, Florida had no tricks left up its sleeve for raising cash. The Everglades had completely failed to pay for itself, and the state was broke once again.

However, the Great Depression kicked off the year following the flood and the federal government eventually saw a works project. It bankrolled millions in relief funds. In the 1930s the Feds built a new dike below and around most of Lake Okeechobee, naming it the Hoover Dike. They also deepened the Caloosahatchee, expanded upon the Saint Lucie canal, and channeled Taylor Creek north of Lake Okeechobee.

These projects actually worked pretty well. Large parts of the Everglades were drained, and Lake Okeechobee could no longer flood. But then things went wrong in the other direction. The Everglades became too dry. The much-valued overlying peat would catch fire and thousands of acres would burn until only limestone remained. Soil blew away like dust in an Oklahoma windstorm.

As if that were not enough, the coastal wells dried up. Florida's cities never piped their water from the Everglades but took it from the seemingly never-ending source of fresh water to be found just a hundred feet below the surface. Thanks to all the successful drainage, however, ocean water had seeped into the coastal wells of the porous Biscayne aquifer. This happened because the aquifer experienced less pressure from the lack of fresh water bearing down on it from the surface. Inconceivably, the southern cities, built on the edge of freshwater wetlands, had no drinking water.

Oops.

The cities—not the state politicians, not the developers, not the Feds—called in the real experts: the United States Geological Survey. Unlike any other agency dealing with the Everglades up to this point, the USGS scientists actually conducted scientific research. They dug wells to see how far the intrusion had progressed, and they discovered that the coast only had one source of water—the Biscayne aquifer. They also realized that all those drainage canals that intersected the coast must be maintained 2.5 feet above sea level, which meant the canals now had to be dammed at their mouths. The new dams, or weirs, would hold the outflow back long enough to raise the water level so there would be enough fresh water to push the saltwater out of the wells. The cities, understandably, jumped on this right away.

By the midforties pretty much everybody recognized Florida was screwed. As if to hit the point home, two hurricanes devastated South Florida in a one-month period in the fall of 1947. Something like 90 percent of the land from Orlando to the bottom of the peninsula temporarily went underwater.

That was it—no more fooling around. The Army Corps of Engineers, up until now just a side player in the Everglades drama, rolled up its beige sleeves. The Corps collected existing drainage data and held public hearings, at which the Women's League reminded them that they were finally making a park out of the unused parts of the Everglades—unused, that is, except by the Seminole, who by that time had so much land granted and taken from them that they had no idea even where they were allowed to be; the farmers told the Corps that all those hundreds of thousands of acres right below Okeechobee must be dry, but at the same time they must have access to water when they needed it; and the developers asked for potable city water and simultaneously more land to develop.

The Corps took all of these perspectives into account and created the Comprehensive Report on Central and Southern Florida for Flood Control and Other Purposes, which it submitted to Congress in 1948. The report outlined the area's

history and competing interests, as well as the massive engineering plans needed to fix the situation, citing primarily the interests of flood control and drainage (evidently the conservationists didn't have much sway). A lot of the report's science came directly from the USGS saltwater intrusion work. Congress, under the Flood Control Act of 1948, thereafter created the Central and South Florida Flood Control Project, authorizing the Corps to implement its solution. After one hundred years Florida's call to "Drain the Swamp!" was finally being answered and best of all, the federal government was going to pay for everything, except for the day-to-day management of the water system, which local municipalities and the state would cover.

Everything up to this point had been piecemeal, inefficient, ineffective, and dangerous. Hamilton Disston's dredging, the state's bombing of rapids and levee building, and even the federal government's earlier involvement with building the Hoover Dike—all were humankind's attempts to improve upon nature, premised on the idea that the entire Everglades was just one big delta, one big spillover that was constantly trying to drain itself.

What the Corps came up with was revolutionary. For the first time ever, the Everglades was seen as one ecosystem stretching from the lakes feeding the Kissimmee River all the way down to Florida Bay, and humans were going to alter it completely.

What was an unpredictable free-flowing system, interconnected throughout 8 million acres, controlled by Mother Nature, was going to be turned into a compartmentalized, completely restricted artificial system controlled by Civilization. All of Lake Okeechobee would be surrounded, and the only way in or out would be through the Corps' canals—a total of thirteen before it would all be over. In the name of safety, development, self-sufficiency, and political might, a thousand miles of levees would be raised—the largest section stretching from Loxahatchee Swamp, in the upper northeast section of the Everglades, to down past Miami. In one fell swoop the coastal cities would be protected. Preexisting over-flow areas would be impounded, including the Loxahatchee Swamp, now known as Water Conservation Area 1 (WCA 1). Below this would be WCA 2, then to the southwest we got WCA 3A, and to the southeast of this was WCA 3B. These reservoirs, along with proper management of Okeechobee, would keep the aquifer free of saltwater, allowing freshwater to travel through the aquifer to the coastal wells, even in the dry season. Hundreds of locks and sluiceways would either contain the water or let it flow, depending on the season and everyone's needs. Then, below Tamiami Trail, the newly formed Everglades National Park, eventually equaling 1.5 million acres, would get whatever passed under the trail. Otherwise, the park was on its own, a mini-Everglades with-out a Lake Okeechobee that mainly had to make do with rainwater. The Everglades Agricultural Area, the 700,000 acres sitting right below Lake Okeechobee, would be pro-tected with even stronger levees. The canals surrounding and crossing it would be improved and a year-round supply of water—but not too much of it—would be guaranteed to the farmers.

Up to this point, only God, and maybe the Dutch, had attempted such manhandling of nature. It was an incredible, socially responsible plan that would save thousands of lives and allow more Americans to make money. This was post-Depression, post–World War II America. We had a right and a duty to increase productivity and improve what was here. And that is what this first Comprehensive Plan set out to do.

A Better Sand Castle

MUCH OF THE CORPS' 1948 COMPREHENSIVE PLAN was simply an improvement upon all the work already done in and around the Everglades and then some. All the old, thoughtless canals were left in place—the Corps simply made them work, sort of like the way you might help a child dig a deeper moat and make a better sand castle, even though you know it's all too close to the ocean.

The Corps' main objectives were to provide water for the farms, reduce the potential for flooding, and prevent saltwater intrusion into the coastal wells; in short, to totally restructure the Everglades. The Corps took what had been a fluid, free-flowing system and broke it down into separate interconnected sections, compartmentalizing an entire ecosystem. It took a while for the Corps to get its dredges in gear, but by the early 1950s, it had machines digging all over Mid- and South Florida from Lake Kissimmee down to Florida Bay. The Corps dug better ditches, built dozens of pumping stations, raised taller and thicker levees, impounded fifteen hundred square miles into reservoirs, and constructed two hundred spill-ways—many with water-stopping gates. The canals now could provide water to the farms as they drained the Everglades; the pumping stations would transfer water from one area to another; the reservoirs would keep pressure on the water table, thus keeping out the saltwater; and the gated spillways, which can be opened to release floodwaters when needed, would take care of anything that might still go wrong. Meanwhile, what was to become Everglades National Park was left alone, except for: 1) the gated spillways that kept the historic flow out of this lower Everglades area, except in times of potential flood; and 2) the bordering canals that made the vast majority of water bypass the park.

To better understand the magnitude of the Corps' hand-iwork, look at pumping station S5-A. It is the second largest pump in the world, located between WCA 1 and the Everglades Agriculture Area (EAA), and powered by six 1600-horsepowered engines that can move 3 billion gallons of water in twenty-four hours. That is three times the amount that flows through the Mississippi River at New Orleans in an average twenty-four-hour period. If you were to stand in front of such an onslaught, you'd be blasted off the planet—well, practically. The Corps has never run all six engines at once, but they're there, just in case.

In case of what? The Everglades transmogrifies into a tsunami? (Currently, the S5-A facility is being converted to a storm-water treatment area that will filter phosphorus and nitrates seeping out of the EAA.)

Anyway, you get the picture. Meanwhile, the Florida Legislature replaced the Everglades Drainage District with the Central and South Florida Flood Control District and infused it with the power to regulate all these new works the Corps would be building. (In 1976, the Central and South Florida Flood Control District was turned into what is still known today as the South Florida Water Management District.)

By 1959 the Corps had successfully divided the Everglades into three sections: the upper Everglades, made up of Lake Okeechobee and the Everglades Agricultural Area; the middle Everglades, made up of the three reservoirs known as the Water Conservation Areas (which did not exist in three distinct sections until 1963); and the Lower Everglades, made up of Everglades National Park. (The Corps didn't begin channeling and leveeing the upper, upper Everglades— the headwaters known as the Kissimmee chain and the Kissimmee River—until 1962, draining some 48,000 acres of wetlands. This drainage was completed by 1971, creating year-round pastureland for Florida's cattle industry.) All of which cost tens of billions of dollars to complete.

You'd think with all this digging and draining completed, it would be time for a celebration, except America's fledgling environmental movement, riding the wave of the antiwar movement, rolled into Florida by the late sixties and early seventies. Without ever putting it in these words, people were realizing that Everglades National Park was too small. Setting aside one and a half million acres for the park hadn't been enough; everything they'd been trying to preserve and save was dying anyway, simply because the park didn't control its water source.

For the very first time the Florida legislature appeared to have some kind of a conscience, thanks to a strong contingent of liberal northern immigrants who liked their water clean and their swamps filled with the sounds of bugs and birds, not airplanes. In 1968, backed by newspaper and magazine articles and a heavy-handed NBC documentary on the demise of the Everglades, the Florida legislature defeated a proposed international airport to be built in the Big Cypress Swamp. (Big Cypress would become a national preserve in 1974, forcing the airport proponents to think farther south.)

Simultaneously a severe drought in South Florida helped clarify the Everglades' fragile position. The park began campaigning for more water. Governor Reubin Askew held a Governor's Conference on Water Management in South Florida in 1971 that announced the painfully obvious: not enough water was reaching the Everglades, and the water that did find its way through the spillways was polluted. The U.S. Congress stepped in and established a new minimum for water delivery for Everglades National Park.

From that point on, it became a constant tug-of-war between the environmentalists and the developers/farmers. A Florida Water Resources Act called for improving water quality to sustain the natural system. The Water District tried to help out Lake Okeechobee by dumping runoff from the farms into the Water Conservation Areas (WCAs); this helped the lake, but ruined the pH-balance of the WCAs and cattails took over. The state protected part of Big Cypress with a preserve. Sugarcane farms grew from a total of fifty thousand acres to four hundred thousand. In 1983, then Florida Governor Bob Graham started a Save Our Rivers program designed to clean up the stumbling ecosystem—from the Kissimmee River on down. The Corps continually issued permits for digging up more and more limestone on the ever-encroaching perimeter of the

Everglades. The ensuing mining pits drained the adjacent wetlands, resulting in more and more loss of habitat for wetland species—from the endangered wood stork to the grunting pig frog.

It's not until 1987 that the Everglades muck really hit the fan. That year the Florida legislature passed the Surface Water Improvement and Management (SWIM) Act. SWIM required the five Florida water management districts to develop plans to clean up and preserve Florida's natural water systems. To the casual, and not so casual observer, the South Florida Water Management District (SFWMD) did nothing. Finally given some real ammunition, the environmentalists turned to the federal government, which then sued the SFWMD for polluting the Loxahatchee National Preserve and the Everglades National Park with excess phosphorus.

"All right, so in 1988 they file this lawsuit," Neil McAliley is telling me one frosty April evening, while we're stranded on Biscayne Bay. The engine on my dad's motorboat has suddenly quit working, and Neil, a former Assistant U.S. attorney in Miami, is taking the opportunity to explain how we got to the present-day restoration effort. "Martinez is governor at the time. He doesn't give a shit about the Everglades, so he lets the South Florida Water Management District litigate, and they go out and hire Skadden, Arps in New York. Skadden, Arps is a scorcher, a total war litigation firm. Up against them is the U.S. Attorney's Office."

Neil's my age, forty or so, but looks and acts more like he's still in college. There's a youthful earnestness about him that more than compensates for his being a lawyer. I'm not the only one who feels this way; my dad and stepmother, who've lived in Miami for the past few years, love him. Everybody mixed up in the Everglades always says, "Oh, Neil. Good guy." Although he's responsible for stopping Miami's former mayor from building a new international airport on the eastern edge of the Everglades, and he's got these liberal genes—his family is an old Coconut Grove family, site of the only liberal hotbed in Florida back in the sixties and seventies—he doesn't tend to side just with the environmentalists. Neil has a Florida history and Everglades library of which anybody would be envious and has spent entire mornings telling me all about every person who's ever been involved in Everglades restoration.

Neil and I have tried to venture together in the Everglades a few times, but different things have gotten in the way—like the wildfires that burned through the southern part of the park in 2001. Instead, we're on a lighter outing—a day on Biscayne Bay in my dad's boat to talk about the 1988 lawsuit. It's a fitting locale since much of Neil's career at the Justice Department was been spent trying to protect the bay; the planes from the proposed airport he helped defeat would have flown directly over it.

Neil, his wife Maricarmen, my dad, and I visit Boca Chita Key, but the harbor is so full of boats we can't dock for more than a few minutes. Boca Chita has a sixty-five-foot coral lighthouse built for millionaire Mark Honeywell back when he owned the key in the thirties and forties; he wanted his boat captain to have a beacon for making the key in any weather. The only problem was that his lighthouse, not found on any charts, was illegal, and the Coast Guard made him turn it off mere hours after it was lit for the first time. Still, it is striking, even if it looks like it belongs in a theme park with its circling veranda and landscaped palm trees fringing the peninsula it sits on. No-see-ums attack us the second we sit down at a picnic table, and we only stay long enough to use the bathroom.

We anchor off another key, swim, have lunch, and then head back to Miami—only we don't make it. We are out on Biscayne Bay in water so blue you want to just bite it, like a baby's belly. Every penis boat imaginable (definition: a turbocharged, thirty-five-foot boat that is grossly long without any usable space) blasts past us, seemingly set on destroying whatever tranquility is left in Biscayne Bay, while we wallow in their wake. I've tried every trick I know to get the boat going but the boat hasn't been used for many months. The gas is flooded with water. While we wait for our tow, Neil entertains and enlightens us.

He's had a few beers but is clearly game to save the day. He knows how being adrift in overcrowded, poolside Biscayne Bay is a literal metaphor for my understanding of Everglades politics. He's going to clear things up.

Neil stands up as if he's walked onstage before a hometown crowd. He clears his throat. He'd straighten his tie, but he's only wearing swim trunks. "None of this is coming from me. I picked it all up hanging around the courthouse in Miami. That's the first thing you've got to understand."

This must be the way all lawyers begin a story—denial of culpability. I nod my head. Neil waxes on. The gist is that the SFWMD spends roughly $3 million putting the screws to the federal government. They litigate every single one of the seventy-odd rules of civil procedure. It is probably the bitterest court battle ever in Florida, until the 2000 election, that is. The lawyers on both sides hate each other—they might even resort to cheating at times. (Neil doesn't say this, but I later learn about some information being "inadvertently" sent to Skadden, Arps that lets them know what the Feds are planning to fight with.)

"They were fighting it out over the basic issue of a state's liability . . ."

"Excuse me, Neil," my dad says, rousing himself from what appeared to be a short nap. "If you're not gonna finish that beer, I'd be glad to take care of it for you."

Neil looks down, surprised to see the beer still in his hand. He hands it to my dad, who downs it in one Shrek-sized gulp. It's getting dark, and all those decadent boats that had passed us on the way out are now returning, slapping us around once more with their wake.

"As you can see, it's pretty ugly—when across the horizon comes galloping Saint George: Lawton Chiles. He's running for governor in 1990, and this whole Everglades mess is everywhere. Apparently, Chiles says one day, 'Well, why don't I just come out and say I'm gonna settle the lawsuit and we're gonna save the Everglades. Why not?' Chiles gets elected and in ninety-one, just after being sworn in, the SFWMD and the federal government have a summary judgment hearing in the District Court. Judge Hoeveler is the most patrician, decent, honorable guy, but he's sort of unswerving. And so you're in Judge Hoeveler's courtroom at the summary judgment hearing, and this is . . . you know how the civil procedure works?"

I tell him that my wife is a lawyer.

"But that doesn't answer my question."

"Okay. No, I don't know."

"Summary judgment is how you resolve the merits of the case where the issues are not in dispute. . . ."

"Uh-huh." This comes from my dad, who I could've sworn was asleep.

"In other words this is a major hearing in the case after three years. The courtroom is packed. Skadden, Arps has all these high-priced lawyers who have basically been working all night and weekends, or whatever, for years. They billed the Water Management District two to three million dollars. *The American Lawyer* got all the billing records, and they discovered that they would all order out for coffee every morning in New York, each cup of coffee is twenty bucks, they'd each get a Danish, that is thirty bucks [actual charges were things like seventeen dollars for a newspaper and thirty-five dollars an hour for someone to make copies]. So this whole thing is like Florida's version of the OJ trial. And there's this David versus Goliath kind of thing, because even though it's the federal government, they are outgunned by Skadden, Arps.

"Anyway, so they're all there in court, the courtroom is packed. Who then shows up, apparently without telling the state's lawyers, but Governor Lawton Chiles! He sits in the back. He just comes in and sits in the back. People probably shake his hand. The judge calls the case, and looking up, he recognizes the governor and he's like, 'Governor Chiles, welcome to my courtroom.' It's a beautiful moment, like visiting royalty, you know?"

"Right."

"One sovereign to the other, and then Lawton Chiles says something like 'Your Honor, may I address the court?' The judge says, 'Of course, Governor, we're graced with your presence.'

"The governor gets up there and he says, 'Your Honor, I think it's terrible that we've been spending all this money fighting over whether to clean up the Everglades because the Everglades belongs to the State of Florida and she is one of our most precious natural resources. I think we should be spending our time and our money figuring out a way to save her. Your Honor, I'm here to surrender my sword, and I want to find out who to give it to.' "

"Does he actually have a sword with him?"

"Yep. And so . . . the Skadden lawyers, who have been working for years on this thing, just crumble. Their heads are not just down. Their heads are hittin' the table—*clunk!* The whole courtroom is stunned. And suddenly Suzanne Ponzoli, the assistant U.S. Attorney in charge of this case, very alertly jumps up and says, 'Your Honor, I take that to mean the State of Florida has conceded summary judgment on all of the merits of the case.' The judge says, 'Well, I think that's true.' And the case is over."

But not really. They worked out a settlement agreement over the following year, which included new standards for water quality and an ability by the state to tax the sugar companies for the cleanup. The sugar industry understandably fought back, and since the settlement agreement was not self-executing, sugar's lawyers filed some three dozen lawsuits to block the implementation of the decree. More lawsuits were filed with everybody, including the SFWMD, pitted against Big Sugar. Ever since, Judge Hoeveler, winner of ethics awards and respected by both Republicans and Democrats throughout the American judiciary, has been overseeing the Everglades cleanup effort, since all the challenges go through his court. (In the summer of 2003, U.S. Sugar and Florida Crystals, Florida's two biggest sugar companies, petitioned the courts to have Judge Hoeveler dismissed after he commented that a recently passed state law allowing Big Sugar an additional ten years to begin cleaning up its waste was "clearly defective" and that Jeb Bush was being "misled by persons who do not have the best interests of the Everglades at heart." The law, flying directly in the face of agreements Florida signed with the federal government, allowed Big Sugar to continue polluting the Everglades with too much phosphorus until at least

2016. Hoeveler was dismissed from the case the following fall.)

To get around failed lawsuits, federal agencies began to petition the U.S. Congress, which passed several acts to move restoration forward. Meanwhile, Chiles created a group called the Governor's Commission for a Sustainable South Florida. He took people from the Miccousukee Tribe, Big Sugar, citrus farming, as well as environmental groups, and he placed Dick Pettigrew, former speaker of the Florida House of Representatives, in charge.

"Dick is a true statesman, and without him, we wouldn't have any kind of restoration plan at all," Neil claims. "Everything has to be a consensus."

And so that's how it happened—how we ended up with the restoration plan as it is today. The Governor's Commission developed a conceptual plan for a Corps-led restudy of South Florida and in 1992, the U.S. Congress authorized the Corps to begin the study, using the conceptual plan as a blueprint.

Neil continues, referring to the 2000 presidential election, "You know that vote-recount election?"

"Uh, yeah."

"Well, my reaction was that this means we are gonna get everything that we ask for concerning the Everglades. When they cut every other environmental project to the bone, the Everglades will be fully funded, and the reason is Jeb Bush is a governor up for reelection. President Bush knows he needs to win Florida, and the Everglades is an issue where the Republicans have been beaten twice in the last decade by being out-greened. Apparently, after he lost his first election bid against Chiles, Jeb Bush said, "I will never be out-greened again. Nobody will ever out-environment me again. . . . He ran a very dumb campaign that first time. He made a lot of dumb statements. His most famous one was when an African American asked him at some event, 'What are you gonna do for black people,' and he says, 'Well, probably nothing.' "

"What?" I ask.

"Well, I think he was being honest. He said, 'I'm gonna do things for the whole people. I'm not just gonna to try to pick out one group to favor.' "

"You know what that sounds like is, um, is umm . . . Warren Beatty in . . . what is that movie?"

"Bulworth?" This from my dad.

Yeah, except Jeb Bush is Bulworth in reverse. Senator Bulworth begins the movie mouthing conservative viewpoints to stay in office even though he's a liberal. He then has a nervous breakdown and only then does he say what he really thinks, like in the black church scene where he says, "We all come down here, get our pictures taken—forget about it. . . . You're not gonna get rid of someone like me unless you put down your malt liquor and chicken wings and get behind somebody else besides a running back who's killed his wife."

Bulworth insults everybody but wins by doing so, if not literally, then at least figuratively. Jeb Bush initially lost by being honest and insulting people and then learned to lie and won. Is that really going to help the Everglades?

The towboat arrives. The driver tosses us a line and drowns out any further conversation as we head back toward Miami. Fittingly, the Everglades, just a few miles west, is lost to us behind all the chaos and bright lights of the big city.

Stolen Water

ALAN FARAGO, A GRASSROOTS ORGANIZER ON STAFF AT the Sierra Club, schedules an educational meeting for me in Miami, a get-up-to-speed-on-the-real-problems-with-the-restoration-plan conference, held on the thirty-sixth floor of One Biscayne Tower. First, though, we meet for lunch a few floors below at the Banker's Club. My father, who works in this building and whose conference room we're using for our meeting, has slipped us in as his guests. It's not the kind of place you'd expect a grassroots organizer to feel comfortable in.

You feel as if you've stepped into some kind of genteel past at the Banker's Club. It's all white linen, plush carpeting, fretting black waiters needlessly scurrying to assist, padded leather chairs on wheels—the perfect props for the overweight good ol' boys you'd expect to find in here. Never mind that in today's Miami this club is filled with Cuban Americans, African Americans, women, and yes, a handful of white males—and none of them need such gargantuan chairs. Overlooking a slough of discount electronics stores, a waterless fountain, and a deserted park, the Banker's Club is where the shakers come to make a quick deal, press the flesh, or simply oil those connections that keep Miami running as smoothly as . . . well, this is Miami and nothing runs smoothly.

Hobnobbers are shuffling around us, padding through the country-club-special carpeting. Alan greets a few of them. Although the chair dwarfs his lean, athletic frame, he's comfortable here. There's something a little slick about him, sort of like he's a jet-setting businessman, which makes some sense given his background. After graduating from college, Alan headed for China in the early seventies, where he taught for a couple of years. Then his father died and he returned home to help his brother run the family's successful engineering firm. Ten years later they sold the business and Alan got an MFA in creative writing at Columbia University. He didn't like the atmosphere in New York or L.A., and recalling childhood visits to the Keys, he decided to move there in the late 1980s. What was supposed to be an interlude, a long vacation while figuring out his future, turned out to be something else because of a fishing trip near Key West.

"I was on my small skiff poling after two tailing permit [a Keys sport fish prized for its long-lasting fights and spookiness]," Alan explained to me. "They probably weighed twenty or thirty pounds each and were flashing their tails in the air as they nosed into the sea grass for crabs. I remember having difficulty getting into a position where I could set my pole down and cast to them. I followed them for a very long time, about twenty or thirty minutes. I became aware, gradually, of a buzzing sound in the distance. It was a pair of Jet Skiers. I was in a national wildlife refuge west of Key West, and it was the first time I'd ever heard them in the wilderness . . . so far from land. The sound grew closer and closer. At the moment I made my best cast to the fish, these Jet Skis wheeled around the corner and ran over my line. The fish ricocheted away."

And it was then that he became the relentless activist he is today. (In 2003 the Everglades Coalition presented him with the John Kabler Award at its annual convention for the work he's done on behalf of the Everglades as a grassroots activist.) Alan wrote articles, badgered the press and eventually succeeded in having Jet Skis banned from Florida's wildlife refuges. During this same time, it became clear to everybody that the coral reef on the Keys' Atlantic coast was dying and that Florida Bay had gone from being a clearwater paradise, carpeted with turtle grass, to a shadowy milky bay destroyed by unprecedented algae blooms which helped create a 450-square-mile area known as the Dead Zone. Pompano, sea trout, and snappers fled their traditional waters and were replaced by mud-sucking catfish and mullet. Alan joined the fight to help these ecosystems and became a part of not only the environmental movement's network but also the greater Florida political system; a successful environmentalist has to be, especially in this land where politics is as staged as a professional wrestling match.

Alan's brought a colleague along. We'll call him Stolen Water, for reasons you'll come to understand. The first thing Stolen Water says to me, glancing quickly around the room before speaking in a clear voice, is: "I have to tell you from the outset. I work for the federal government, and I'll be there many more years. I need my job. I'll deny everything."

Stolen Water is a credible source. He has negotiated with officials from Justice and Interior, as well as many state agencies and organizations. His record is clean as a whistle. He looks me clear in the eyes, and as my lunch goes uneaten, describes, in detail, a series of broken legal commitments, questionable decisions, and outright lies perpetrated by the federal government—all in the name of water.

"What we learned is that the SFWMD documented the degradation of the Everglades Agricultural Areas for more than ten years before the federal government sued them. They had scientific proof that the pollutants from the sugar industry were altering and destroying the Everglades. They did nothing about it. U.S. Attorney Dexter Lehtinen filed a lawsuit against SFWMD in 1988 for flooding the park with this stuff. Instead of saying, 'Oh, yeah, you're right, we've got the information, here it is,' the District suddenly hires the most litigious, greedy, nasty law firm in the world, Skadden, Arps. Justice battled them for three years until mid ninety-one, when they entered a settlement agreement that looked good for the environment. In order to make the consent agreement binding, agricultural interests were given a role; they were granted the right to litigate. Well, by ninety-three, Sugar said it'd deal. We had them on the ropes!"

Up to this point, Stolen Water's account pretty much corresponds with Neil's, with the added bit about the SFWMD sitting on the info for ten years. "The subsidized Sugar Program was coming up for reauthorization, and suddenly the Interior Department took over negotiations. It became an absolute disaster. There's nothing to read about this, but there were definitely phone calls to the White House and this lame deal was cut. Although we had to settle, we were as obstinate as possible, so they snuck around us and the court threw it to the Florida legislature, which is controlled by agriculture and Sugar. The result of all this is the Everglades Forever Act, which is the very basis for the Comprehensive Everglades Restoration Plan."

I can buy that the Department of the Interior crumbled, as poorly funded as it is. Justice caved because of heavy political pressure? It's not hard imagining where that came from. It's on record that in ninety-six, Alfy Fanjul, co-owner of the Florida Crystals sugar company with his brother Pepe, called Clinton while Monica was visiting. It's also public knowledge that Fanjul hosted fund-raisers for Clinton and introduced him to the Florida Cuban-American community. He even visited Clinton's Interior Secretary Bruce Babbitt with Big Sugar's plan for the Everglades ecosystem. Soon afterward, Babbitt announced the Clinton Administration's plan for restoration, which bore an uncanny resemblance to Big Sugar's, and in 1995 Babbitt's office supposedly at Fanjul's urging quit litigating the then five-year-old legal quagmire that Stolen Water (and Neil McAliley) have described. Stolen Water believes he's proof that the Comprehensive Plan is politics as usual; he was told by his bosses to back down from trying to reach a settlement with any teeth in it. If the original consent decree overseen by Judge Hoeveler were followed, the Everglades would be a whole lot cleaner.

I remember my untouched food and try to wolf down a little bit before our meeting. Stolen Water disappears into the crowd.

Alan and I go upstairs where a few others are already sitting around a long oval table overlooked by bold windows through which we can see the turkey vultures coasting on city thermals. We've got Hal Wanless, a rumpled professor at the University of Miami and head of the school's geology department. Barbara Lange, the Sierra Club's spokesperson on mining in the Everglades, who works with Alan. Stuart Pimm, professor of conservation ecology at Duke University and the world's foremost expert on the endangered Cape Sable sparrow, has not yet arrived.

I'm still trying to process what I think Stolen Water has just told me when Hal, a pleasant enough fellow whose voice would have sent me facedown in college, begins talking about going up to the state legislature recently at the behest of the Sierra Club to ask questions about the proposed Aquifer Storage and Recovery system of 330 new wells.

"There's a water problem here. Everybody knows that. But eagerness for these new wells is overriding the science. While I'm not a groundwater expert, I've talked with my friends who are. They're getting grants and contracts provided by the state, so they're not comfortable talking about this publicly; their livelihoods depend on staying in the state's good graces. But most of these scientists don't think this new storage system has been studied anywhere near enough. . . ."

Stuart Pimm arrives and Alan starts talking about the history of the Sierra Club's involvement, explaining that the Sierra Club was the only big environmental group to go against the Comprehensive Everglades Restoration Plan (the Comprehensive Plan). Then Stuart, the protector of the tiny Cape Sable sparrow, jumps in, with Barbara occasionally interjecting, essentially, that the Army Corps of Engineers is a force of evil. She's the Sierra Club's point woman concerning the ongoing limestone mining allowed by the Corps in what has become the Lake Belt region—a series of mining-pit lakes strung along the eastern corridor of the Everglades. About $1 billion of the Comprehensive Plan's money is going into developing these pits as water reservoirs. The Corps is scheduled to grant enough permits to mine an additional twenty thousand acres to aid in developing more reservoirs for the Everglades.

I'm taking notes, checking my tape recorder, watching them wave their arms frantically, and soon my head is spinning. Pimm, short and contented-looking, with thinning hair and wire-rimmed glasses, has the kind of face that wiggles and squints when he gets agitated, and right now he's highly agitated. Years ago Pimm got together a group of scientists to write a letter to Babbitt explaining that the Comprehensive Plan wasn't, well, comprehensive—that it didn't provide enough guarantees for water being delivered into the natural system. Needless to say, he was ignored.

"Listen, this plan is being set up so that the Corps is judge, jury, and executioner, and meanwhile the Pimm Plan is being ridiculed as the Let Her Rip Plan! Well, their plan doesn't appear to have any ecological restoration. It doesn't provide guarantees of water into the system. If you look at their Web site, it sounds wonderful, all this talk about restoration, but then you go to where they direct you for details and there's nothing there!"

It must be his British accent, but I swear he's floating in his excitement at the other end of the table, airlifted à la Mary Poppins. Isn't real restoration occurring somewhere? Or am I just being snow-jobbed like everybody else?

"There's no restoration," Stuart says. "You go to this front page, and it tells you all the wonderful things that are going to happen. And you go, Wow! And of course, that's all most people do. And let me tell you, if you want to go beyond that, you cannot. It will say decompartmentalization is the key to the entire project and you think great, and you go and type in decompartmentalization, and it never appears again. It's just not in there. Will Florida Bay get enough good water? No. Will Everglades National Park? No."

"We're fighting in court to get them to raise the Tamiami Trail right now," adds Barbara. "A longer section of it."

"They're never going to do it," Stuart contends.

"But it's in the plan," I try.

"This is what they're going to raise—a small gap of a few thousand feet."

I think out loud to make sure I get it: "So right now there's no plan to really raise it. Why did I think there was going to be a substantial change?"

A big smile crosses Stuart's face. "Because they said, 'We're going to raise Tamiami Trail,' but in the small print it's only a few feet—God, I wish I had my maps." He continues on to another point which he believes also illustrates the lack of real restoration. "Look, they've got this decompartmentalization of 3-A and 3-B they're touting. It's on their Web site. And they've got these wonderful weirs dotted along the map. They're not going in until 2035, and they're only going to be seventy feet wide. That's minuscule when you consider how large these conservation areas are. Although other areas above there might get opened up, it's not going to flow because of these small, useless weirs. In the meantime they're going to build hundreds of miles of new structures. And they can't do any of that until they've completed Mod Waters, which is a completely different project."

Some more background is in order: Back in December of 1989, President Bush the elder signed into law the Everglades National Park Protection and Expansion Act, authorizing the purchase of an additional of 107,000 acres of the east Everglades for the park. The act also directed the

Corps "to construct modifications to the Central and Southern Florida Project to improve water deliveries into the park and shall, to the extent practicable, take steps to restore the natural hydrological conditions within the park." It looked good on paper, and the park did expand eastward, but a small number of inhabitants living in what is now known as the 8-½ Square Mile Area refused to budge. These landowners include small-scale Cuban-immigrant farmers, as well as second-home weekenders. Mod Waters, the second part of the park protection and expansion act, has been waiting fourteen years for them to sell so flow to the park can be improved. The inhabitants burn presidents and governors in effigy and don't appear to be going anywhere. Apparently, the Corps can't, or won't, begin other environmental restoration until Mod Waters is underway.

"Mod Waters can't be done until this, this, and this happens, and it's a long series of if, if, if, for restoration. Whereas, if you look to the structures that they're building for water supply, they're already bragging that they're going to complete them in 80 percent of the time."

The meeting continues for a while longer, but I've gotten the gist. The Comprehensive Plan sucks. The Corps doesn't care about the environment. The Everglades is still going to die.

Wonking the Wonk

S O I GO SEE DR. EVIL HIMSELF, STU APPELBAUM, THE Comprehensive Plan's program manager at the Corps. His offices are far removed from the Everglades themselves, located outside of South Florida in the Corps' Jacksonville headquarters in a squat, monolithic federal building, just a few blocks from the Saint Johns River, my adopted manatee's stomping grounds and currently Florida's slowest-moving river, slower even than the Everglades because the Everglades no longer exists as a river.

I'm sent up to the correct floor after the security guards confiscate my tape recorder (this is in March 2002, six months after 9/11) and wander the halls looking for the right office. I enter an area labeled Environmental something or another. It's an auditorium of cubicles and desks. I ask the closest cubicler where Stu's office is. "Appelbaum? What section's he in?" the guy asks.

Slighted for Stu and the Everglades as a whole, I respond "Everglades Restoration" as crisply as possible.

"Oh. He's somewhere over in the corner, back there, I think."

Stu, when I finally find him, isn't what I'm expecting. I'm expecting: a fat man, dressed in polyester, with a gnawed cigar dangling from his mouth, or perhaps an inflexible military man with a jutting locked jaw and no-nonsense attitude. He is neither.

He looks nervous but committed—like he's being shoved into battle. He's dressed casually in a checked button-down shirt and khakis. I think there's a pen in the pocket.

It all feels awkward: the fluorescent lights, the cold office, the formality of an interview. I'm anxious about asking the right questions. He seems equally anxious to be heard correctly, to be understood.

I start off with some easy stuff, finding out he's forty-eight, been in the Corps for twenty-four years, graduated from New York Polytechnic in 1975 and George Washington University in 1982 with a master's in engineering. He came down to Jacksonville in '88 and first worked on the Kissimmee River Restoration Project from '90 to '92. Then in 1993 he moved to the Restudy.

I ask how he got involved.

"This was basically an assignment. However, I moved here from Washington to get involved with some more interesting projects, like the Kissimmee. Saw it as a great challenge—you don't get something like this very often in government work: a chance to make a difference. That notion—of doing something historic, something to be proud of—has driven us from the beginning. I've got people who've been putting in sixty- to seventy-hour workweeks for many years now."

Again, not what I expected. My curiosity piqued, I ask him if he's a big outdoor person, thinking this might explain his enthusiasm. He just laughs. He is not an outdoor person. He's from Queens.

Thinking the ice has been broken well enough, I blurt out, "Stuart Pimm says there's no restoration to the restoration plan."

I don't think he's expecting this. He adjusts himself in his seat before speaking and then says slowly, carefully, "The Everglades has lots of issues, lots of problems. It doesn't lend itself to sound-bite science." He pauses. "I'm disappointed with what Dr. Pimm is saying. I think it questions our motives and desires. He's not right. Obviously, there can be a lot of opinions about things, but I get concerned when people question our motives. We're on the cutting edge of the Corps here. We're held up as the role model. It's not often you get a chance to make a difference, to do something your grandkids will be proud of."

Stu explains that his guys spent six years working on the Comprehensive Everglades Review Study and that their goals were to balance the needs of the natural system with water storage for urban areas and agriculture. "The question I have for people is, do we want to recover as much as we can or do we just want to have a natural area? If you removed everything, it would be natural, but it wouldn't be the historic Everglades. So what is the desired end? Recovery, which we're hoping to bring about with the Comprehensive Plan, or simply more natural?"

I don't know this at the time, but later I find out that

Stu's synopsis of Congress's instructions to the Corps regarding the Everglades isn't correct. Liking Stu, I don't think it's his fault but is simply how information was passed down to him.

Somebody, whether it was somebody back in the Clinton Administration, or in Florida's Senator Graham's office, or out on a two-hundred-foot yacht parked off the Bahamas, convinced the Corps that the effort should not be about restoration but about balancing all the needs of South Florida. Was that somebody right?

Wondering these things, I later stumble through the legislative history of this morass, specifically the 1992 and 1996 Water Resources Development Acts, in particular section 528(b) of the 1996 Act. What I learn is that the Comprehensive Everglades Restoration Plan was really supposed to be about restoration and not just another extraordinary feat of civil engineering. Back in 1996 the words were very clear. Congress actually required restoration of the Secretary of the Army: "The Secretary shall develop, as expeditiously as practicable, a proposed comprehensive plan for the purpose of restoring, preserving, and protecting the South Florida ecosystem. The Comprehensive Plan shall provide for the protection of water quality in, and the reduction of the loss of fresh water from, the Everglades." The 1996 Act goes on to say that the plan shall also "provide for the water-related needs of the region, including flood control, the enhancement of water supplies, and other objectives served by the Central and Southern Florida Project." According to those who know more abut these things than I do, strict statutory construction tells you that because providing for the water-related needs of the region appears after the request for restoration, it is clearly secondary.

Why should we call it a restoration plan if it's not really

going to be restored? Because Congress told the Army that they (and we) wanted a restoration project.

Only, they didn't get it.

Yet, even so, Congress accepted the plan and passed the Comprehensive Everglades Restoration Plan as part of the 2000 Water Resources Development Act. Are our representatives in Congress so easily duped or did they get what they really wanted? Everyone in the House and Senate gave it a "Yea," except for one lone Republican senator from Oklahoma, Senator Inhofe, who didn't vote no because he loves the Everglades but apparently because he is opposed to the U.S. government owning or maintaining public lands.

During the interview, Stu says Pimm needs to talk with the Corps, that they'd be more than happy to meet with him, hear his concerns. I'm pretty shocked to hear they've never had an eye-to-eye meeting. And admittedly, I've come to Jacksonville to make Stu squirm, thinking that the Corps cares nothing for the environment. Now I'm not so sure. I feel a bit like a Ping-Pong ball, but maybe I'm getting a clearer picture.

I ask Stu if he'll meet with Pimm and Alan Farago down in Miami. He readily accepts. Later, I ask Alan and Stuart and they agree, too. We meet a few months later, back at One Biscayne Tower, same long oval table. Stu brings along Nanciann Regalado, a former Audubon activist now working for the Corps as head of its Everglades Outreach Program.

"The reality is that the Comprehensive Plan has become a very complicated process with endless numbers of working-group meetings. Ordinary people aren't set up to participate at that level," Alan begins immediately after we've all just sat down. "So while I agree with the notion that it's important for us to meet today, you guys are pretty

fixed in the direction you're moving. You've got the pro-grammatic regulations coming out very soon and that's going to be a real watershed event for all of us. Everything turns on that."

The Corps Web site explains: The programmatic regula-tions "will establish targets and timetables for deliveries of water to the natural system and for ecosystem and habitat recovery, including targets for water quality, habitat acreage, and species diversity and abundance and provide for the development of quantitative benchmarks for other water related needs of the region, including flood protection."

Translation: The programmatic regulations *are* the Comprehensive Plan. When the final draft of these regula-tions is made public in 2002/2003, pretty much everybody with an interest in restoration, including the Sierra Club, the National Audubon Society, the National Wildlife Federation, and the World Wildlife Fund, denounces them. Some of the reasons are: The Department of the Interior, federal steward of the properties to be restored, is given no authority or con-trol over the project; no ecological recovery targets are stated; and the independent science review panel, mandated by the Comprehensive Plan, is toothless since it has no inde-pendence from the Corps.

Back at the meeting Alan brings up more current issues that are upsetting to the Sierra Club, namely, the number of permits being issued for mining in the Lake Belt region and the stagnant Mod Waters. "This gives us a lot of doubt about the way things will go in the near future," Alan says. "When I heard that Nanci was going to be here, I was actually very pleased about that because I remember when Nanci was working for National Audubon. The buffer zones was such an important part of your work, Nanci, back in '94 and I'd sort of simply ask, 'What's happened to the buffer zones?'"

The idea was to create a buffer between development and the Everglades, an area on the eastern edge of the Everglades that would be free of development and/or mining. Instead, there's the ever-growing Lake Belt mentioned earlier.

Alan continues. "And now, here we are a few years later, and we have a plan that includes pumps that are far in excess of capacity with respect to the historical needs of flood control in that area. We have more permits. Everglades restoration has turned into a flood/supply project. And we know you guys are under tremendous pressure from all of these municipalities who seem to be drinking the drain right now. And we know that the local people simply want to build more self-storage units in the wetlands. So that's my reality, my world."

"You know I've been in this for a long time. . . ." Nanciann begins. "As long as you have. I personally would not be sitting at this meeting if it weren't important for us to hear and to listen and to talk and try to react. If there's any way that you want to tell us to engage with you in the future, we'd be glad to do it, Alan, because I swear it's really important to us."

"Can I call you on that?" Alan jokes, then adds, "Let's talk about the 8-½ Mile Area. I don't know how you solve that particular kind of problem through public education outreach. I mean the meetings were there, the people were burned in effigy. . . . The problem is that we've got this incredibly technologically intensive plan with a lot of scientific uncertainty, and we're not sure about the good faith or the goodwill of the Corps and other government agencies to look at viable alternatives because any discussion of viable alternatives has been shut up, shut off, and frustrated."

"But if you have a plan that is constantly changing and

you're saying it will change, then we are changing," Nancy points out. "This project can always change. We can say, okay, that after review by NAS [National Academy of Sciences], this high-tech solution isn't working, you really need lower-tech, and the Corp is saying that they are willing to do this. . . ."

"What has been hijacked here is not the depth of management—it doesn't have anything to do with the depth of management—but the flexibility," Stuart Pimm says, wading in. "Nothing we're seeing represents any sort of major assessment of any alternative hypothesis, and it strikes me that there are some fundamental things here that are wrong; not least of which is the very notion of the Aquifer Storage and Recovery system. . . . Why I think this process is fundamentally not scientific and why the scientific community, outside of Florida, is critical, is because you don't see other alternatives."

Instead of dumping all 1.7 billion gallons of water each day into the ocean, as they currently do, the Corps and the South Florida Water Management District (SFWMD) plan to pump it into South Florida's aquifer. Their method? Those Aquifer Storage and Recovery wells, 330 to be exact, that are being incorporated into the existing matrix of water-control structures. Basically, 1.6 billion gallons a day will be injected 1,100 feet underground with new, high-powered pumps, where, theoretically, it will push aside the naturally brackish water, forming a kind of freshwater bubble. This bubble of Evergladian nectar will simply hang out until it's recovered for agricultural use, drinking water, and even recharging the Everglades.

Sounds great, except that no one's quite sure if it's going to work. Of the current one hundred municipal underground treated-wastewater injection units (similar to the proposed new wells for the Everglades) in use in Florida, 33 percent leak into the aquifer. The National Research Council, a consortium of independent scientists from across the country, warned in 2003 that the limestone that seals in the aquifer may fracture because of the rock's frangible nature when those new wells are used.

Stu Appelbaum says that if the new wells prove ineffective or destructive, the Corps will turn to another solution and then Stuart Pimm counters by suggesting they skip the wells altogether and simply buy more land.

"To substitute for the historic Lake Okeechobee overflow, you can either go to this very dodgy technology which is going to take a very long time to work through or else you can buy the land needed," Stuart Pimm says.

They argue about surface storage and evaporation, each group discounting the other's point or information.

At some point Stu Appelbaum says, "When you talk about additional surface storage, you're not talking about an East Coast bumper because there's nothing left, really. I mean we went through this whole exercise in trying to outline what is left and—"

"Every piece that is left, we need," Alan jumps back in. "That's the point. We've got to do something to clean the water that we have. It's an enormous problem. It's also a big problem that you guys are separated from the regulatory end of the Corps because it's hard to know how we're evolving. Are we going to get to a greener Corps before our time runs out on the Everglades? I mean there's twenty, thirty years before the ecological changes will begin. How much mischief is going to get done in the next twenty or thirty years?"

While Stu and Nanciann might represent a greener Corps, the Corps' regulatory office is just as cement-gray as it's always been. Alan's concern, and it appears to be valid concerning such projects as the Lake Belt area, is that the regulatory office is still a tool of development—that it's not affected by the Comprehensive Plan. It's issuing permits for mining and development as if this were still the good ol' days of the four Ds—dredge, dam, dike, and divert.

"One of the things I was hoping to do today, " I intercede, "was make sure everyone is understood. So I wanted to just go back to L-67. Your major concern is with the weirs that are being suggested versus just taking it out completely, right?" I ask Stuart Pimm.

L-67 is the levee that separates Water Containment Area (WCA) 2 from WCA 3. As mentioned earlier, Stuart thinks the planned weirs are too small. I turn to Stu Appelbaum and ask: "But is that on the table for the Corps?"

"I think it's still on the table," Stu says. "What I would say is when the Restudy was done, that issue was looked at with a view toward taking it out, because we don't disagree on that. We had a team that was working on decompartmentalization. We'll need to look at that again and maybe some things could change or somebody may have a more creative solution but I don't think we have a difference in value on that."

"No?" Stuart says, "Good, then."

"I don't have an emotional attachment to any of the structures that are out there," Stu continues. It's a good line, one that I end up hearing him say on a number of occasions, and he appears to mean it. "It's relatively inexpensive to take structures out. To backfill and take those things out, that's one of the cheapest things—clearly a lot cheaper than developing the Aquifer Storage and Recovery system. That's not the issue for us, and I can tell you that the managers love decompartmentalization. I mean, they want let-it-rip because when it's passive, it's not their fault. But there's an ecological trade-off between different areas of the system."

"Absolutely."

"So here we are, asking the scientists and the various resource agencies what we should do, and we're getting conflicting viewpoints. Obviously we've got to make some decisions, opt for something that's going to upset somebody. Going in to this in 1993, I would have bet that we would have had the biggest debates among the trade-offs between human needs and the natural system and how we were going to reconcile that, but the most intense debates have really been among the different ecological aspects—about upstream versus downstream."

"Your scientists are saying to you that if you open up L-67, you're going to destroy 3-A essentially, but then you have Stuart, who's telling you that you've got to open it up because you're going to keep destroying the Everglades farther down south. Is that right?" I ask.

"Or you have scientists in the park that believe that flow is a very important criterion, maybe the most important, and others that believe that restoring the water depths is more important than the flow," Stu adds. "Of course, in an ideal world, you get both. But if you can't have both, which is more important? Those are the kinds of debates that have taken place and probably will continue to take place."

"I have a different take on this," Stuart Pimm says. "I do not see that there are credible major scientific disputes about what decompartmentalization will do. If we all agree to restoring flow, then let's *really* restore flow and see what happens. At some stage of the game you've got to sit back and ask, 'What's the system supposed to look like?' For instance, a big issue would seem to be the large pumps that

118

you want. Is there anything that you guys can say that's reassuring?" Stuart asks.

"356?" This is a pump station set up to protect the 8-$\frac{1}{2}$ Square Mile Area along the park's eastern border. It may send high water into the nesting area of the Cape Sable sparrow during the dry season, which is also the bird's nesting time. The sparrow nests in marl grass less than a foot above the waterline, and the unexpected high water might contribute to the continued decline of this endangered species.

"You are essentially setting up a situation where you will do serious harm to an endangered species," Pimm says. "I have already written the biological jeopardy opinion that I hope the Park Service will eventually adopt. And the service's position is that they can't do anything—it's sort of like—a lot like somebody who waves a gun at your head. You know the police cannot arrest him until he shoots you. This is a pump with no other express purpose than to flood the hell out of North East Shark Slough."

"Guys, I have to go across town," someone says and it's over. Everyone's been heard, but I'm left wondering to what end?

After the meeting Stu e-mails me some answers for Stuart. Why go through me? I think they just forgot to exchange e-mails, but I can't help thinking this also explains the past and doesn't bode well for the future.

Stu: "With regard to the L-67 extension. I was wrong in saying that it will not be degraded until the end of the Mod Waters project. In fact, we have already let a contract to remove the southern end of it now (as part of the IOP for the sparrow) rather than waiting to do it as part of the Mod Waters project. I understand that some interests are not happy that we are proceeding with removal now. The removal should be or is about to get underway very shortly. Bottom line—removal of the L-67 extension will happen. Some of it now, the remainder under the Mod Waters project."

Okay, so I'm thinking, "Great, the meeting served some purpose. Communication has helped. There is some help. We can believe Stu."

Stuart thinks otherwise.

"As long as I've been working in the Everglades, the L-67 extension has been on the verge of being removed," he writes back to me in response to Stu's e-mail. "One fine day it will happen, so making my doubts look foolish. Quite how much will be removed will be interesting."

Stu also wrote: "With regard to the size of the S-356 pump station for the Mod Waters project, the pump size that will be constructed is smaller (about half the size) than what was originally authorized under the Mod Waters authority." So, essentially Stu is saying that Stuart's Cape Sable sparrow will not get flooded out of existence when water has to be pumped into Northeast Shark River Slough.

Stuart: "Yes, but why now? This was to be part of Mod Waters, something the Corps is in no hurry to implement."

Stu: ". . . the Corps and SFWMD have committed (I believe in writing) to use the additional capacity only for seepage management, not additional flood control. The change in sizing and the assurance about the use of the capacity have been agreed to by DOI, the Army, and SFWMD, although some at Everglades National Park are still concerned about the potential for increased flood protection."

Stuart: "Abundant evidence shows that the Corps builds things only to use them and use them at their full capacity."

A River Runs
through Some of It

THE STORY OF THE KISSIMMEE RIVER IS THE STORY OF THE Everglades' past, present, and what could be its future. Today, it's an example of what the Army Corps of Engineers can do when the right pressure is applied.

The Kissimmee, flowing out of the chain of lakes that was once the beginning of the drainage system for the Everglades, was a slow meandering 116-mile river, teeming with life. It could have been the "poster" river for a subtropical wetland ecosystem. It had everything from snail kites to wood storks to oxygen rich waters creating life wherever it flowed. At highwater some 50,000 acres of wetlands attracted birds from across the Americas and produced perhaps the best largemouth bass fishing in the country. Then, thanks to cattle interests and the political fallout from continuous flood damage, the Army Corps of Engineers stepped in during the 1960s and forced it into a fifty-six-mile ramrod-straight canal. Birds disappeared, plants and fish died, and it began to look like what it was, a depressing drainage ditch, surrounded by ghostly S-turns—the old riverbed filled with muck. The Corps finished its handiwork in the early 1970s for $29 million. A few years later, however, the state realized what it'd done and began a restore-the-Kissimmee movement, but it was not until the 1992 Water Resources Development Act that the federal government gave the South Florida Water Management District (SFWMD) and the Corps the go-ahead to return a portion of the river to its natural state, which it is currently doing for $524 million.

The Kissimmee River Restoration Project is a joint project between the SFWMD and the Corps of Engineers, but it is the SFWMD that performs the studies that create the blueprint for restoring the river. The SFWMD conducts all testing to measure oxygen levels and water quality and ensure the river can sustain indigenous fish and plant populations. It's the SFWMD that tells the contractors the Corps has hired how to move dirt so as not to damage the environment any further. Essentially, unlike its role in the greater Everglades restoration effort, the SFWMD is keeping the Corps in line; at least, that's how SFWMD sees it.

"The Corps is good when talking about 'dike it,' 'dam it,' 'dredge it,' 'drain it,'" Paul Whalen tells me as we load our canoe and kayak for an overnight trip down a restored section of the river. Paul's head of the Kissimmee project for the SFWMD and we've met up at Riverwoods, the SFWMD's Kissimmee headquarters. "Even to this day they'll say to us that it's easier and cheaper to dig a straight canal, and we have to say, 'No, that's not what we're doing. We're restoring the environment.' " However, in 1983, the Corps of Engineers, not SFWMD, began the first backfilling demonstration project to test restoration techniques on the Kissimmee—techniques now being used—so this might just be a lot of spin.

Besides a charming willingness to speak his mind, Paul is refreshing in other ways as well: He has arrived with his own kayak and dry bags and is clearly comfortable and competent in the outdoors. While leading our boats, he begins spouting facts and figures about the river, discussing the pros and cons of the Kissimmee River Restoration Project while tying perfect bowlines and tight trucker hitches; doesn't let up the entire day. It's fun to be around a bureaucrat who actually cares about his job, and the same goes for the publicist Bill Graf.

Bill, a forty-seven-year-old, former award-winning reporter-columnist turned flack for SFWMD Orlando District has spent days setting up our outing. It's to be a day on the water with Paul and Bill, a night camping along the river with Bill, and then a morning's paddle back to Riverwoods. Bill has shockingly white hair and a continual half smirk, half gullible look that is both unsettling and charming. Over the phone and now in person Bill makes a distinction between bullshit PR and reality by saying things like, "What I'm supposed to say is . . . but what's obvious is. . . ."

The Kissimmee is the SFWMD's and the Corps' big PR tool. They've blown up a water-control structure—dam, to you and me—and returned natural flow to fifteen miles of the river, and they plan to bomb another structure and open up a total of forty-three miles of meandering river while filling in twenty-three miles of the fifty-six-mile-long Kissimmee River canal. More than half of the canal will remain as a necessity for maintaining flood control. I'm reminded by different SFWMD staffers on many occasions that the whole environmental restoration world uses the Kissimmee's restoration as an example of the good that government can do, environmentally speaking, while still providing safe living conditions for its citizens.

We drive to the put-in near the headwaters of the newly restored river, less than a few hundred yards from the old S-65B water control structure—the one they blasted apart a year earlier. We haven't even started paddling when Paul becomes animated about the changing landscape that surrounds us. "Look at all this dead stuff, will you! Isn't it great?" he calls out, pointing to a mass grave of withering myrtle that can't handle the influx of fresh water. "We love this dying myrtle—none of it would've been here if not for the canal, and now it's going away." Now that this section of the canal has been filled in and the river is once again flooding the surrounding plain, exotic plants brought in by the cattlemen over the past century are either dying on their own or being poisoned by airboat patrols loaded with herbicides.

Something's not right about the spot, though; it doesn't seem natural to me. We've driven down a dirt road over some flat cow pastureland, and suddenly there's this shallow water right in front of us spreading into a tangle of trees and bushes. Where's the river?

Then, slightly embarrassed, I realize that I'm the one that's skewed. This is natural—or at least natural looking. I'm so used to channeled streams and rivers—ones contained by humans in one form or another—that initially I can't place this environment. This is what a drainage basin looks like—no clear put-in, no definitive water's edge. It just spills over until it no longer can.

We shove off in about four inches of water, and Paul

starts up again. Paul just can't stop going on and on about the restoration project, even as we paddle past . . . hey, wasn't that a wood stork? Aren't they endangered?

"What?" he asks. "A wood stork? Yep, they're already coming back. Who would've thought it'd happen so fast. Before restoration, you wouldn't even see a great blue heron. Now we've got wood storks."

Not only are Bill and I having a hard time—okay, impossible time—keeping up with Paul physically, at first, I'm also having a hard time catching up to him in the enthusiasm department, too. We've passed a couple of those herbicide boats, and although I know they're necessary, they do make me wince a bit. Also, the fact that this restored section of the Kissimmee is adjacent to an Air Force bombing range and that the restored area is only fifteen miles long has initially left me, well, unexcited. But his joy is infectious, or maybe it's merely the recuperative powers of nature, but pretty soon I'm as jazzed as he is, glad to see the dying live oaks and rejoicing in the pickerelweed scraping against my hull. This river actually has a current. In the shallows you can see the bottom, which is changing from muck back to sand. Fish are jumping and slapping the water all around us. Kingfishers, wings beating a breeze into the still air, dive for their breakfast. I don't feel like I'm in any Central Florida I've ever known. It feels undeveloped—not just a little ironic considering the hundreds of millions of dollars that are being spent to develop this river back into a seemingly undeveloped place.

A little later we reach a bend in the river that has more glossy ibis resting on its marshy banks than there were birds on the entire Kissimmee River before restoration began. They make a terrible ruckus as we land our canoes a hundred feet downriver. Lou Toth, chief scientist at SFWMD for the restoration project, is sitting on an airboat, waiting for us. He's got long wavy hair and a good tan, not a bad-looking poster boy for this poster restoration project. For some reason, Lou brings to mind that Steve Miller Band song "The Joker": "Really love your peaches / Want to shake your tree / Wooo-Woooo."

Lou's the one person who has seen this project from beginning to end. SFWMD originally put him out here to do some standard studies, not expecting anything unsettling. This was back in the late 1980s, when SFWMD's main concern appeared to be how best to keep Big Sugar happy. In the old guard's mind, they probably shouldn't have put Lou on the case, because he starts turning in so many right-on reports that go into the public record that the state has to do something about the river. So I'm looking at a demigod of Florida restoration, and I feel a little bit like Lou knows it. Or maybe he's just tired of doing interviews; I've seen him quoted in many publications, from *Wired* magazine to *The Washington Post*.

Lou takes us off the river's channel, crossing into a fledgling wetland prairie. We stop in less than a foot of water surrounded by typical broadleaf marsh flora: arrowhead, lilies, pickerelweed, maidencane, and willow. "Not much more than a year ago, this was all Bahia grass, pastureland. Cows, exotic grasses, and fences were everywhere," Lou says. "Very rarely did you see ducks and wading birds." On command, a flock of glossy ibis passes overhead.

I mention to Lou that I've wanted to travel the entire system, pretend I was a drop of water in the Kissimmee and travel through Lake Okeechobee, then into the canals and reservoirs of the Everglades Agricultural Area and then through the saw grass of the park, finishing up at Florida Bay. He looks at me as if I'm the biggest rube he's ever seen. How could anyone do that? he's wondering. It's nearly two hundred miles with no campsites. Farms and cities all around. In the saw grass you'd be lucky to make six miles in a day. If the mosquitoes don't eat you up, some bear, snake, crocodile, alligator, or panther will gladly finish the job.

But that's not what Lou's look means, it turns out. My idea is even dumber than that.

"A lot of people talk about doing that, pretending they're a drop of water. Some have even tried it," he says, smiling a bit. "But the water from the Kissimmee really never makes it out of Okeechobee into the lower Everglades or anywhere near the National Park. It's all either used up by the farms or dumped into the ocean by all our canals. The Everglades Agricultural Area is really the place where the Everglades water comes from."

Ah, the Everglades Agricultural Area—that seven-hundred-thousand-acre area least understood by the general public, yet the very heart of the matter. The EAA is not only home to the sugarcane farms and citrus plantations but also site of some of the compartmentalized water conservation areas that have people like Stuart Pimm so upset. This is where many environmentalists are waging their battle. The EAA, they claim, puts the lie to the word *restoration*. It doesn't matter how great you make the Kissimmee or how clean the water is in the park if something isn't done about Lake Okeechobee and the EAA.

The most interesting thing I learn from Lou is that I stayed at the traditional headwaters of the Everglades the previous evening when I was in Boggy Creek Basin. Imagine that: There I was in an expansive Ramada along an endless strip mall just south of Orlando, surrounded by multiplexes, McDonald's, Wendy's, Publix, Mobil gas stations, Long John

Silver's, Wal-Mart, and Kmart, and I had no idea that the sewage-ditch-like waterway between the massive roads was the traditional headwaters of my beloved Everglades.

Soon after Lou departs, buzzing off into the sunset, Paul leaves Bill and me beside an old growth stand of live oaks, part of a reclaimed cattle farm that now serves as a campsite. Paul has to get back to the office. (Interestingly, and I think tellingly, Paul is let go a few months later, and I hear it's probably because he bad-mouthed the Corps one too many times. Then, in September 2003 Lou Toth is fired from his position on the Kissimmee River project after making public remarks that he was "discouraged" by delays in the river project. SFWMD's explanation was that Lou, employee of the year in 2001, made "unduly disruptive" statements to the media.)

Bill and I, unaware of these men's future fate, pitch a tent, break out the beers (Bill's off duty), and don't talk Kissimmee or Everglades restoration for the rest of the night.

Bill went to so much trouble preparing our dinner before heading out—chopping vegetables and chicken, marinating all of it in sherry and sesame oil, packing condiments—that it caused a little marital friction. He'd been borrowing spices, frantically getting everything ready, and had just started to pour the last of his wife's special sesame oil into the marinade when she cornered him in the kitchen and asked, "Okay, what's going on here? I've never seen you work so hard on a meal. Is there another woman?" And she had good reason to ask; the meal, cooked Boy Scout–style in a "pot" made from aluminum foil, is perfect.

And so is the evening. Although most of the river is, and will remain, a canal, this little swatch feels like how I imagine it must have always felt. At night the calls of the returned birds and other animals are deafening. I'm woken up three or four times to what sounds like deranged laughter, and I can't help thinking that, yes, we deserve being laughed at. But watch out; there's no telling what we might do next.

The Kissimmee might be a riverine palimpsest, where works are created and then destroyed, but underneath it all there remain a lot of answers.

Bill sets up another Kissimmee River day for me a couple of months later so that I can witness a day in the life of the river's scientists and hands-on saviors.

At 5:30 A.M., in the middle of March, Stephanie Melvin and I head out to listen for and count birds. A thick, sweet smell hangs in the air. I'm running around in the dark, asking, "What's that smell? What's that smell? It's so lovely." It's from the orange blossoms, trees that wouldn't even be here if it weren't for the old canal days. Stephanie has short blond hair and reminds me a lot of the manatee scientist Ann Spellman. She's attractive but not soft. She's wearing jeans and a light gray shirt and could be a scientist in a movie—good-looking, no-nonsense (think Anne Heche). She's a senior environmental scientist specializing in wildlife ecology, masters in wading birds.

We zip down the river by airboat into a fledgling broadleaf marsh, stopping in a half foot of water. The mosquitoes are hungry and happily find me wearing shorts.

"This is where we did baseline counts. Now we're doing post-restoration," she explains. She starts banging her Palm Pilot. "I just started using this thing." She punches some more buttons, nothing happens, and she sets it down.

"Okay, what I do here is a six-minute survey—you need

to be very quiet so I can hear them," she says. I'm a little startled that birds are counted by their call and not by a visual sighting, but if you know your bird calls, she explains, hearing a bird is a lot more definitive than seeing one. So, for the next six minutes, she calls out what she hears to Ken, the tall, lanky manager of SFWMD's Riverwoods headquarters. Ken is driving the airboat for the morning and recording all the data.

This is how it goes.

"Common yellowthroat—fifty to one hundred (feet). Northern cardinal greater than one hundred. Common yellowthroat greater than one hundred," she calls out. She's listening so intently, her binoculars unconsciously held up to her right ear. "What is that?" she asks, slightly annoyed. "Okay. Red-winged blackbird fifty. Common yellowthroat greater than one hundred. Common yellowthroat greater than a hundred. Sedge wing less than fifty. Marsh wren less than fifty." I eventually learn how she uses the data: if the bird is within fifty feet she can estimate the mean abundance—how many there are. If it's greater than fifty feet, she uses the information to help create a species list.

It's more than just beautiful, this listening so intently to a bird's call—it elevates the birds to an exalted position. This must be the attraction to birding—the missing link I've never understood. All these crazed birders out there aren't getting excited about *seeing* a little ol' common yellowthroat. It's all about *hearing*. They give voice to nature. Virtuoso performances in a world of virtuosos. I've listened to birdcalls before but never so intently, and today I'm hearing something else—a distinct message from each bird, declaring its vitality.

"Bittern flying over." She looks with the binoculars. "Common moorhen fifty to one hundred. Green heron fifty to one hundred. Okay. It's cool that the hens are actually singing—instead of just chirping," she whispers. "They're so cute. I just love them. They're so curious—not at all afraid." All right, maybe she does have a soft side. The moorhens *are* cute, along with their cousins the black coots, unless, as someone points out later, you consider how they cannibalize the excess fledglings in a flock (mental note: must remember not to anthropomorphize nature). They have multicolored bills—yellow tipped followed by a bright red that ends near the top of their heads.

Stephanie has worked for SFWMD for six years. This is only her third month of fieldwork since restoration. However, she also did three years of fieldwork *before* restoration, coming out like this every month, counting the birds by listening. Some of the most important counts are of the red-winged blackbirds, the sedge wrens, and the common yellowthroat because they are most common in marshes. If they're back in high numbers, then restoration is working.

"In areas that were pastures, we're already seeing a significant increase. I mean, in the past I never saw any there and now I do," she says. The biggest difference has been in the different sections of the recovered river—Pools A, B, and C. "When we first came out here after restoration and did aerial surveys, I was like, 'Wait! Wait!' There were just so many, we had to come up with new ways to count them. There were six times the number of birds."

We speed along to a few more sites. We hear, besides the birds I've already listed, eastern meadowlarks, mourning doves, white-eyed vireo, tree swallows, sandhill cranes, a yellow-rumped warbler, a crow, lots of black-crowned night herons, double-crested cormorants, great egrets, purple gallineaus, and great blue herons. A northern harrier gets

"That's cool. Awesome. Never seen one of those here before," as it glides over our heads.

We see seven white ibis standing at a bend. "Look how pink their faces are. Their feet and faces get bright pink when they're ready to breed," she explains. Then we see a pair of mottled ducks. "They're our only endemic marsh duck. An increase in them would be great and we're seeing that. I know this guy who was out here three years prior to restoration and didn't see a single mottled duck."

After about three hours we head back to Riverwoods. Stephanie doesn't stop counting the birds, even though the official count is over. When we disembark, she says, "There's a lot of warblers around," and she mimics their call. They seem to answer back.

Next I'm handed off to Dave Colangelo, thirty, and Kim Kanter, thirty-two, who measure dissolved oxygen and oxygen saturation levels in the restored section of the river. They're like a comedy routine. Dave says something serious and then Kim straightens him out. "Come on, Dave. You were laughed at. Teased. Picked on. In front of everyone. Admit it," she'll say, and he stares at her like he doesn't know what she's talking about.

We pass a section where the channel has been filled in, but I point out that there's a gap in the riverbank, like something's knocked it down to get into the new marsh. Dave complains that some airboaters probably did it.

"Aw, man," Kim says, "you're guilty of it too, Dave."

We travel to different water-monitoring stations. At one the oxygen-saturation level shocks them both. It's 93 percent. "I've never seen that," Dave says. "That's so high. The organisms using the oxygen are not depleting it. Previously, we were only seeing 50 percent saturation. That's a huge change." A greater oxygen-saturation level means a healthier river. You don't have those dreaded algae blooms. The water is moving. You have a lot of healthy, happy fish. At another site the gauge records 99 percent saturation, and the dissolved oxygen figure climbs to 8.87. At another it's 9.0.

"Some of this improved dissolved oxygen is seasonal," Dave cautions. "So it's not like the river is all restored and everything. In the winter our concentrations are high like this, and in the summer they'll drop down. When there was no flow here, the DO was always under five. Five is the standard for healthy fish." So 9 is unbelievably good.

I push Dave and Kim on their opinions of the Corps, asking what it's like to work with them. Are they the Boogeyman or not? "They come out here, go real fast in their big rigs," Kim says. "They have no regard for anything."

Dave's a little more circumspect. "They tend to be difficult, like they have all the answers, but they did a great job filling in that canal," he says while we're tied up to a gauging station, eating sandwiches for lunch. "I don't see them out here, though. Besides us, I mostly just see USGS people."

An alligator floats by. We see its nostrils, then its eyes and brow and a little of its dark tail.

"Man, there's one thing that always bugs me," Kim says, pointing to our alligator. "Why are alligators always painted bright green in pictures? They're not green. How'd that ever start?"

We check another station. It records 100 percent saturation. Dave seems a little stunned. "Things aren't restored here yet, despite these figures," he says, almost defensively. "The floodplains should have water in them 90 percent of the time. We haven't had anywhere near that yet, but I'm really looking forward to doing some fishing this summer out there. This used to be one of the best places to go bass fishing in the world."

"In the world? Are you sure about that? In the world?" Kim chides. Dave just shakes his head. She's from Florida; he's from Connecticut. Dave, sporting extended sideburns and longish dark curly hair, is a bit of a modern-day hipster. Kim is definitely more down to earth. Dave is a Doors fan—went to The Whiskey in L.A. just to see where Morrison started. Kim isn't telling me what music she likes. She might like the Doors, too, but definitely wouldn't bother going to some bar just to see where some alcoholic flasher got his start.

The last gauging station is back where the channeled river takes over—Water Structure 65-C. There's no discernible flow here, and it's choppy from a strong wind that's blowing, much as it'd be on a lake, as opposed to a real river. It's a depressing place after being on the remanufactured "real" thing. But there's a surprise: The DOs are really high: 8.6 at one meter, 7.5 at 6 meters. The previous week they were only 5 at 6 meters. "It's probably the wind," Dave says. While they're recording their readings, I wonder what would it take to get rid of this water structure, too. They've already blown up one successfully, so I don't mean explosives-wise. I mean politically. Then, happily, unexpectedly, I remember this one will be blown up, too.

It's all so absolving. Destroying humankind's mistakes to revive nature, restore some balance to the most unbalanced system in America. I start to wonder, as we motor back to Riverwoods, what about Lake Okeechobee? Can't we just blow up the Hoover Dike as well? It's a beautiful sight—watching these structures destroyed to save a natural environment—as if Edward Abbey's Monkey Wrench Gang has taken over the world. My time on the Kissimmee brings to mind Abbey's wilderness guide's lament: "Hell of a place to lose a cow. Hell of a place to lose your heart. Hell of a place . . . to lose. Period."

"Let her rip!" as Stuart Pimm says. Just tear it all down and let the water flow. Why not?

Where's the Ice Cream, Honey?

T HIS IS THE SECOND LARGEST NATURAL LAKE IN THE United States. Lake Michigan is the biggest. This lake is twenty-seven miles wide and it's thirty miles long. It's a very shallow lake. Its average depth is ten feet under a fifteen-foot pool. Right now it's about fourteen, so it's about nine feet deep, except for your waterways and canals."

Don't worry—I didn't understand the part about the depth, either, and at least you're not sitting next to this kid who evidently either stepped in a pile of dog poop or did something in his pants that he hasn't told his parents about. The kid is wearing ear protectors over his Walkman headphones, even though we're still at the Roland Martin Marina dock with the engine off. Roland Martin is this world-famous fishing guide everybody's heard of—everybody who watches those bass-fishing shows on cable TV.

I'm taking an airboat tour of Lake Okeechobee. Our guide continues undeterred by the fact that he's making no sense whatsoever. "The lake is also an Intracoastal Waterway, which you can see those big boats taking advantage of. You can cross the state of Florida by boat by using this lake. You can go to the Atlantic Ocean, start out there, and come all the way across and go clean to the Gulf of Mexico. So all the big boats that you see at Roland Martin Marina are just commuting, they're just coming through for a stopover, then they're going on to their destination.

"I want to tell you a little bit about all these dead trees so you don't think we've got a lot of disease on this lake," he goes on, pointing to a stand of gray trees that stretch to the horizon along the lake's southern perimeter. "About eight years ago the State of Florida came up with a tree restoration program for here and the Everglades, and one thing you want to remember is Lake Okeechobee is the headwaters for the Everglades. Anyway, they targeted two trees—the melaleuca trees and the Australian pine. They are not native, so they came in here and they killed them all, but there's a good side to that story. Two years ago, they planted seventeen thousand new seedling trees. They planted swamp apple, custard apple, and water maples. They are all seedlings and they're just now growing, so we won't see a lot of them, but in the next few years we'll see a lot of new tree growth on the lake.

"Now, I'm going to tell you a little bit about this old dike behind you. In 1926, 1928, this dike is not here. They had two big hurricanes. The one that is the worst is in 1928. The surge of the storm took most of the water out of Lake Okeechobee and put it in the surrounding areas and drowned between

2,500 to 3,000 people. Herbert Hoover is president then and says we need to do something about Lake Okeechobee. We can't let that disaster happen again. They said what we're gonna do is we're gonna go around the edge of it and dig a ditch, and this ditch is this canal on your right and your left. They dug this ditch all the away around the lake, took the dirt up and piled it up and made a dike, and of course it's called the Herbert Hoover Dike, and its sole purpose is to contain this water if there ever is another hurricane like that again."

Our guide looks like an airboat tour guide should. His skin resembles a worn pair of cowboy boots. He's as skinny as a blade of saw grass. And he seems as bored as shit. I don't know about the other folks, but I'm sure glad I've tossed in thirty bucks for this.

He cranks the motor, and before gassing it into the deafening stages it takes to make an airboat movable, he lets us know how the tour is going to progress.

"If I see anything of interest, I'm gonna kind of holler at you real loud and you kinda want to watch where I'm turning it in because maybe there'll be a gator or whatever—you never know what you're gonna see on this ride. The other day we seen some manatees, we hadn't seen them for a while. . . . So put your headsets on, here we go."

The airboat revs up. We speed through the canal and then we quickly skid left into the lake proper. An airboat doesn't turn like a boat because it has no rudder in the water—it's more like an airplane. This makes the airboat an awkward vessel at start-up and a little slippery on tight turns. The rpms are let loose to a deafening pitch, and if the boat also has to make a turn, you might as well forget about hearing for the rest of the day. And as far as bird-watching goes, let's just say it makes a lot more sense to me now why the biologists, who only travel by airboat or helicopter, don't see very many birds in the Everglades. My brother-in-law runs a bird-scaring company that sells canons and handheld bang-guns to help farmers and airports wage war against the aviary world. His family makes good money off these noisemakers, but his arsenal is nothing compared to an airboat.

The lake is a little spooky on this southern edge with its ghostlike poisoned melaleuca trees creating a barrier to the rest of the lake; I call this edge Dead Forest Standing. Our guide doesn't tell us this, but melaleuca, native to Australia, were first introduced to South Florida in the early 1900s. The reason the Corps originally planted these melaleuca along Okeechobee back in 1940 was to reduce wave action after the devastating floods. Floridians liked them back then because they have an evapotranspiration rate six times that of saw grass—in other words, they could dry up the Everglades. Some wacko tried seeding the Everglades from an airplane in the thirties with this purpose in mind. Floridians don't like them now because they do such a good job of using up water and stealing the habitat of indigenous trees that they have taken over nearly 20 percent of South Florida's wetlands. Various government agencies have been trying to eradicate the stubborn trees for decades now without much luck. Poisons don't do much good. Fire makes them release more seeds and doesn't even kill the standing trees because of a thick spongy bark that insulates the inner structure. These days the USDA has been releasing imported Australian bugs, psyllids, and weevils that kill seedlings. Supposedly, the bugs won't prove harmful to other species.

Our guide does his best to stay on the airboat trail, blasting past saw grass, cattails, Kissimmee Grass, and a fringe of banana plants, so named because of their resemblance to banana tree leaves. He almost stops when a couple of us point out a bloated, eight-foot alligator, floating dead on its back, but then thinks better of it. (He'd probably have to explain that it was killed by an airboat and then consider that maybe a craft racing along at 50 mph isn't such a great thing in an endangered ecosystem.) Eventually, when we're well clear of the dead alligator, we stop.

"If it's real hot out, alligators tend to not lay as much on the bank because it gets their skin so that they don't like it, so a lot of them will lay toward the edge of the water," he says, hopefully scanning the banks. It's all about seeing the big animals—alligators and manatees. If a guide can show you just one of them, then it's a successful trip. "This is where we seen the manatees the other day. There was two of them together. We followed them all around and watched them, but this is also a good place to see a lot of alligators sometimes. You can come in here at nighttime with a light and shine it, and them old eyes just light up like a light."

We start and stop one more time. We pass two alligators, but we're going so fast, they don't look much different than floating logs of melaleuca.

That's my introduction to Lake Okeechobee. To be honest, I hadn't been expecting much more. I've gone on a handful of airboat rides around Florida by now, and they're all the same. The driver gives a quick, down-and-dirty intro, we're told we'll probably see alligators, and then we speed around for about an hour or two looking for them. At some point the driver stops and talks about how awful the sugar industry's been, how it and the Corps have ruined this paradise, but now "we're saving it." This is standard issue airboat-guide talk. Usually, we travel in a not so big circle until we see a couple of alligators. People are satisfied if they see their alligator, although their presence is a true indicator of only one thing: We're not hunting them to extinction anymore. It indicates nothing about the health of the Everglades, Lake Okeechobee, or the Loxahatchee Wildlife Preserve—another one of the places I've visited in an airboat. At the end everyone walks off the airboat saying things like "Wasn't that great. I wasn't expecting to learn so much. . . . Where's the ice cream, honey?"

Everything I've read about modern Lake Okeechobee has painted a pretty bleak picture, so the airboat tour seems fitting enough. One year algae blooms, caused by too much nitrogen from the dairy farms, kill millions of native plants. Another year there's too much phosphorus. Then, for a while, the lake is too high because of massive rains, and emergent plants die off. Then, another year, perhaps too much water is let out and the lake dries up so much that the Corps and the SFWMD suddenly have to haul out pumps to balance the lake and Water Conservation Areas so that the saltwater doesn't enter the freshwater well fields on the coast.

Of course, it wasn't always like this. How different it was, though, we're not too sure because no one surveyed the whole south rim of the lake before Disston started to drain the lake. No photographer catalogued the shoreline. It wasn't until the Army chased the Seminoles through the interior that white men even successfully traveled to this lake. Before that, it was called Lake Mayaca, a name left over from the time of the Calusa.

As a result, no one really knows how the Okeechobee spilled into the Everglades. Most accounts agree that the lake didn't simply spill over in a vast sheet of water, but that it flooded, or trickled, depending on water levels, through many rivers and streams into what became—a mile, three hundred yards, five miles down—a wide plain of water.

There is a somewhat obscure account, though, of this shoreline, from 1883. Back when newspapers sponsored Great Expeditions, like *The New York Herald* sponsoring Henry Morton Stanley's search for Dr. Livingstone, the New Orleans *Times-Democrat* sent a group of soldiers and adventurers to explore the beginning of the Florida Everglades and traverse its entire length—from Lake Okeechobee down to the Gulf of Mexico. It's a hair-raising, pain-filled tale of suffering through the saw grass. At first it doesn't even appear our explorers will be able to get clear of Lake Okeechobee:

"The Gulf of Mexico never presented an angrier appearance, or waves rolling higher, than what we have experienced and seen for the last three days upon the waters of Lake Okeechobee, an inland sea about fifty miles in length and breadth, with nothing to break the force of the wind or waves until the water-covered swamps of the Everglades, which form its shores, are reached.

"The water is too shallow near the shore for the larger boats, so we are compelled to stand out from shore about half a mile, while the smaller boats and batteaux keep in the grassy waters, which extend for about an hundred yards into the lake around its whole margin. In an hour after our departure from camp we find ourselves sailing along the southern shore, peering anxiously for a spot of dry land on which we can camp and dry the contents of our boats. After traveling about eight miles, we discern with our glasses a white sand beach backed by quite a forest of large trees, and immediately signal the other boats to follow, and sail for it. On reaching it we find a high strip of land about a mile long and fifty yards wide, a beautiful white sand beach, and in the rear a little land-locked harbor in which our boats can lay perfectly protected from the wind. It is, indeed, a perfect piece of good fortune to find such a resting place, and as each boat is borne by the waves through the channel to this little bay, which lies calm, still and quiet, quite a contrast to the war of the waves from the lake as they dash upon the shore but a few yards off, the men give a hearty cheer. Allen's canoe, the 'Judson,' capsizes in getting through the channel, losing all our knives, forks, cups, plates and some of the cooking utensils. Mr. Harlander, our artist, suffers the same fate, so far as the capsizing is concerned, but loses nothing. Mr. Phillips, our commissary, ships a sea, and comes very near sharing the same fate . . . for half an hour there is a perfect fusillade in camp, each man trying to see how many alligators he can kill in a given time. The whole surface of the water is dotted with these monsters from three to ten feet and over, who perhaps for the first time have seen a human face, for unconscious of danger, they come swimming from all directions, never stopping until they get within a few feet of the guns. . . . We name this beautiful little bay 'Kitty Harbor,' and in time, when Lake Okeechobee shall become one of the thoroughfares of commerce, many a vessel will find refuge from the angry waters of the lake, and here rest in perfect security. . . ."

Comparing this account to my own little foray onto the lake by airboat where we never even get to the other side of Dead Forest Standing compels me to contact Bill Graf, the SFWMD publicist, to find someone, preferably a scientist, who might want to paddle or sail across Lake Okeechobee from the mouth of the Kissimmee to the south of the lake at Clewiston and discuss the lake's issues.

Bill, wanting a fishing vacation I believe, produces Dave Swift, a scientist and town council member from Royal Palm Beach. Dave, a big man, has a small boat called a flats boat made for scooting across South Florida's shallow waters in pursuit of game fish, and he has huge ice chests.

Besides being a local politician, Dave also works for the SFWMD. He worked on the first SWIM plan—a SFWMD study that was done to analyze the lake's algae blooms mentioned earlier. He knows the lake and its issues better than anyone, and more important, he has the right boat for a couple of lazy days on the lake.

Unlike the canoe trip we took together on the Kissimmee, this is Bill's idea of heaven—a speedboat, lots of fishing poles, and some nighttime libations. We'll ride around in Dave's boat, do some fishing, and talk about the lake. Liking the tone of our outing and figuring this might be as close to paddling Lake Okeechobee with a scientist as I'll get, I accept.

After jetting across the southeastern edge of the lake, we rumble to a stop in a break of saw grass. There's a quality to the air, a primordial heaviness, that pushes you back in time to the days before drainage—if you just gaze north and can ignore the smoke of the sugar refineries and their high towers, jutting above the levee in Belle Glade and Clewiston, and also ignore the boat's plastic deck and comfortable swivel chairs. When you're looking this way, you can't see the thirty-five-foot-tall impounding levees or the thirty-two manmade water outlets that ring the lake. Instead, you see a miragey surface of water that stretches as far as your imagination with waves of heat rippling above the surface, hiding something mysterious that could be approaching you at any moment—something that's gonna grab you from behind and make you disappear forever. *Okeechobee* is the Seminole word for "Big Water" and that's what it is. Plain ol' BIG.

I feel small but not in a bad sort of way—just less than this ocean of fresh water. I like this feeling. It reminds me of how I felt in my grandfather's arms, whose nickname was also "Big." It's that same kind of feeling you get when you're on a boat in the ocean. Everything seems possible. I could light out across the lake and slip into another world.

I'm looking at this big water and can't help wondering for the umpteenth time why the farmers below the lake can't be bought out and a more natural flow returned to the Everglades. Isn't that exactly what we all think is going to happen with a restoration plan? It's what we're expecting, right? Right?

FADE OUT.

The Battle Against Evapotranspiration

A Short Screenplay

FADE IN:

INTERIOR. BEACHSIDE MARRIOTT INN DAYTONA, FLORIDA

The camera pans from partitioned room to partitioned room of a substantial conference hall where we see PANELISTS discussing and fighting over current Everglades issues. Everyone is represented: BIG SUGAR, the CORPS, the SFWMD, even the SAVE-THE-APPLE-SNAIL splinter group. This is the big annual Everglades Coalition Conference 2003.

The camera rests on four panelists sitting before a CROWD of 100. They look nervous but confident. The camera pulls in close on JUANITA GREEN, president of Friends of the Everglades. Juanita has taken over the mantle from Marjorie Stoneman Douglas. She, like Douglas, used to be a reporter. Juanita has not given up on recreating the Everglades' natural flow, or sheet flow, as a solution to the Everglades problem. She's not on the panel but sits one row back, watching.

The PANEL CHAIR begins the discussion. The topic: "Is ET a problem for Flowway?" (ET means evapotranspiration, and flowway stands for the historic sheet flow that once characterized the Everglades river course.)

The camera turns to STU APPELBAUM, the U.S. Army Corps of Engineers leader of Everglades restoration. Stu's not supposed to be here, but a guy who works for him has ducked out. Stu, once again, has to explain why there'll be no return to a more natural flowway. Stu looks different than when we last saw him. He's wearing black. He seems more confident, looser.

STU   Back in the nineties, when the Corps of Engineers and the SFWMD performed its Everglades' restudy, it considered restoring complete flowway to the Everglades—in other words, buy out the EAA sugarcane farmers, tear down the dike, and let her rip. The flowway alternative was not considered beyond the reconnaissance study for a number of reasons, and the primary one comes from the question, "What do you want flowway to do?" Do you want flowway from the shores of Lake Okeechobee on down through the Everglades? That can't happen. Unfortunately, the topography today is very different than it was historically. The Everglades was a very different system over 150 years ago. Today we have tremendous soil subsidence in the Everglades Agriculture Area, and to a lesser extent elsewhere. If you look at the Farm Earth Foundation exhibit—it's one nice exhibit and I'm not just saying that just because there's pictures of me out there. . . .

Appreciative laughter.

STU   What you'll see among that class photo is a marker showing the subsidence. You can see the level of the land at different dates. It really gives you insight into how significant subsidence has been. It's taller than me. If you were to try to flow water through the EAA, it wouldn't flow. Could you store the water there and pump it farther south? Of course you can. In fact, we have the Everglades Agricultural Reservoir, which is now scheduled for sixty thousand acres, recommended as part of the restudy. But I don't care whether it is a ponded area or surface reservoir or a lake, you have evapotranspiration. It's a fact of life and our modeling accounts for it.

Stu goes on. We hear him in the background as we cut back to Juanita, listening closely, taking notes, getting visibly madder. Then, a ROUNDISH, EARNEST MAN raises his hand a few seats away.

ROUNDISH MAN I'm not worried about the accuracy of the model on the flowway. I'm worried about when we can look at the models and see if they have any bearing on the Corps' decision to abandon the flowway project or is it just because of earlier evapotranspiration theories?

STU Well, evapotranspiration was not the only consideration in rejecting the flowway idea. The plan that has gone to Congress did not contain the flowway, and at this point there are no plans to resurrect the flowway, so our modeling is only looking at sixty thousand acres in this new EAA reservoir. We took what I thought to be a conservative approach in the restudy. The reason was that we've heard a lot from agriculture. They didn't think any reservoir EAA was needed at all—zero acres. We came up with a different answer.

Nervous laughter. Stu appears to be losing the audience.

STU One of the things that the team is going to be looking at is if they can go deeper. Can they go eight feet, ten feet, twelve feet, and what's the trade-off on seepage management and the cost of that versus larger size? I personally am optimistic because I think it will be able to go deeper than six feet. I can't base it on any curve or data; it's just a gut feeling I have that we took the conservative approach.

Juanita's had enough. She stands up, hand raised.

JUANITA The reason we have this panel on ET today is because every time I asked either the Corps or the District about why no flowway, the first thing I heard was ET. Too much loss through ET. That's why the title of the panel is *Is ET a Problem for Flowway?* I know that there are other objections, too, but I would like to have an answer. Once the modeling was done, was it from the standpoint of water storage or was it from the standpoint of ecological restoration, that the no flowway decision was made?

Stu sighs. He's clearly wondering how many times he's going to have to answer this.

STU If you try to flow water through the EAA, obviously you're going to have a problem with the fact that water isn't flowing. If your goal is to create a more natural system, creating a system that then has to be pumped out doesn't do it. . . .

JUANITA Then why did you look into flowway at all?

STU Why?

JUANITA Yeah. Why?

STU Again, because the scientists recommended flowway as a possible solution, and we looked at it as part of the restudy.

The sound of a hundred trays falling to the hard kitchen floor next door shakes the room with its thunder, but Juanita doesn't flinch. Her turn is over, though, and Stu turns to his next inquisitor.

FADE OUT.

Dammed

BACK ON THE LAKE WE'RE FISHING IN A NARROW CANAL bordered by banana plants, a water species with leaves resembling those of a banana tree. I'm just tossing out my line to pass time, not expecting much luck. I make a sweet, arcing cast just to the edge of the growth— only it doesn't stop at the edge. It sails on and on, way past any hope of retrieval. After I've tugged on the line in silence for quite a while, I admit my predicament to Dave, who slowly edges us closer to my snag. Suddenly a large predator thrashes out from under the thick green brush, heading, I believe, right for me. Only I'm wrong. It's a great blue heron, awkwardly gaining altitude to escape the real predators.

Dave looks pretty frustrated. I've read plenty of counter-

153

arguments to the evapotranspiration theory that claim, essentially, that the evaporated water will come right back down from its own rain clouds, and I've pointed out these counter-arguments. This isn't what's bothering Dave, though. I caught the only bluegill of the day a few hours earlier and he's got nothing. Bill hasn't caught anything, either, but he seems pretty content. Happy just to be on the lake. I take this opportunity to ask Dave how the lake has changed since he's been working for the District. Are there more birds? Fewer?

"I couldn't tell you. It looks pretty much the same as it always has. One year it stayed low for a very long time, around eleven feet, and we had flocks and flocks of scaups. They wintered over at the lake. Other times there's hardly any." Lesser scaups, a common waterbird in southern waters, should be found in the thousands on Lake Okeechobee every winter.

Picking up on what I think is Dave's conservative bent, I ask him what party he's affiliated with. He says he's an independent but doesn't elaborate. He goes on, though, about the situation on the lake, and I realize it's not politics making him reticent but instead, the lake's complicated nature.

"When you have a drought, most of the Everglades is dry. Lots of wading birds come to the lake during the dry season, and they wind up utilizing the lake more so it's kind of hard to say how things are affected here. One of our board members has this saying, 'You know, you guys worry a lot about birds, but they vote with their wings every morning.'" Meaning, I assume, that the birds are fine and don't need to be taken care of.

Bill looks a little worried. Despite his I-don't-give-a-shit manner (Note to SFWMD: a manner only displayed to me because he knows I appreciate it), he's a damn good PR guy. He knows how this sounds. The District is supposed to care about the environment these days, but the District is run by a board and whoever is governor replaces the board. You have a conservative governor, you get a conservative board. You have a conservative board, you get a conservative District administration. You have a conservative District, you don't get much conservation. So Bill chimes in, "We're out there to count them flaps, too."

Frustrated, I wonder aloud what the lake's big issues are, if it's not bird conservation.

"It's just not that easy," Dave says. "You've got to look at the past—all that we've done." He pauses. "Look, let me take you over there." He points to some islands a bit to the west. Okeechobee has many small islands along its southern edge, but none in the middle. We head over, zipping through over some reedy Kissimmee Grass, and toss our lines out.

"Back in the sixties and seventies," Dave continues, "these islands were farmed because the lake was down significantly lower than it is today. They grew corn and they had fish camps. And the lake fluctuated roughly between twelve and fifteen feet for quite a while. Back in '78, because of growth in Florida they increased the schedule up to about seventeen feet to provide everyone with enough water. That didn't work, either—too much for the levee system to handle. We had a big issue a couple of years ago about some huge discharges into the Caloosahatchee. People were in an uproar. 'Why didn't we make discharges earlier?' they wanted to know. Well, our guy sitting in a room over in operations is legally responsible for whatever happens, and he has to be authorized by the court to open a gate. He didn't have authorization to open it any earlier, only when he did. We've been toying around with different water regulation schedules for as long as I can remember. If the lake goes up or down in the wrong season, wildlife can't adapt. If you go up really fast, you'll kill the apple snails and knock out the snail kites' food source. But, look, the real problem is that this lake has become the major water storage reservoir for all of South Florida and it's too small. It's that simple."

"Do you think that should be resolved through Aquifer Storage and Recovery or a water buffer zone?" Bill asks.

"It doesn't really matter. There are three things that need to happen. Storage, storage, and storage . . . Where the hell are the fish?"

"What are we fishing for?" I ask. What was I thinking, that if I knew what I was looking for I'd be able to tell Dave where they were?

"I'm looking for bluegill. Let's go up there. Get in the shade."

A minute or two later we're floating under the branches of some fig trees. Over on the island stands the largest fig tree I've ever seen. It could hold a good-sized house and still have room for Swiss Family Robinson. Something about its vast ribbed trunk and branches belong to another era, back when such mammoth trees were everywhere in South Florida. Someone's built a camp around the tree. Handwritten signs warn all to keep away. Evidently its still being used for hunting and fishing.

Bill's trying to disentangle his lure from a willow branch, and Dave's answering some question I don't even remember asking, gesticulating almost angrily across the water. "The lake is a slave and has many masters. Two million acres of the Everglades are either developed or farmed, so when you have a big rainfall the natural storage features of that system aren't there anymore. As a result, the lake is the backup water supply for all of South Florida. Ag looks at it as their livelihood—that if they don't have water, they are never going to have their crop. The fishermen look at it, they want to have a clean lake and have water levels to allow the vegetation to grow and the bass fishing as good as it always was. The storage issue is very difficult to explain to people—that we don't have places to put the water, but we wish we did."

I really want some simple answer about the best thing to do—for the lake, for the farmers, the animals and the Everglades—but each faction competes with the other to such an extent that there is no simple answer, if you are bent on compromise, that is. But isn't compromise what's gotten us into this current mess where we're spending billions of dollars on something that's supposed to be about one thing—environmental restoration—but is beginning to appear more and more like something else—water management?

"Look, a hundred-year-old problem is trying to be addressed by a $7.8 billion plan," he says just above a mutter as he reels in his empty line. "And I run into other guys who have retired and they say, 'We were talking about that thirty years ago!' And you know, they're right."

He says this so casually that I have to prod him. Doesn't this frustrate him even a little? The same thing going on and on, for thirty years, and still going on even though this $8 billion plan has passed Congress?

"Well, actually, I'm the person who discovered this nutrient problem out in the Everglades," he responds. I believe he's referring to studies done by the District in the late seventies that involved introducing phosphorus and nitrates into a test site in the Everglades—a site I'll stumble upon on my upcoming saw-grass trip. Excessive phospho-

157

rus and nitrates are the by-product of the sugarcane farms, cattle ranches, and the like. "I wrote a report in 1982 that these nutrients had moved into the system. It sat on the manager's desk for five years. At the time two District board members were sugarcane growers, and they didn't feel that the time was ripe to be discussing these things."

His understatement is killing me. Water quality has been the major battle ever since. Essentially, the sugar industry (and cattle and citrus to a lesser degree) does not want to abide by the Everglades Forever Act nor foot the bill for cleaning its own refuse. Back in the early nineties, most scientific reports indicated that the phosphorous count needed to be dropped from the average 270 parts per billion (ppb) levels that were continually recorded coming out of the Everglades Agricultural Area to 10 ppb. The Everglades Forever Act required the farmers to meet this new level by 2006. Only then will the water be neutral enough to sustain periphyton and saw grass—which in turn sustain every other living organism that is the Everglades. Without periphyton (that mustard-colored spongy world full of algae and microscopic creatures that filter the Everglades), the river of grass becomes the river of cattails. The original consent decree of 1992 (that became the basis for the Everglades Forever Act) and The Comprehensive Plan also called for the level to be lowered to 10 ppb by 2006, but in the spring of 2003, Florida legislators voted to change that date to 2016, "or the earliest practicable date." Who's to say they won't just make a similar vote again in 2015 or that the earliest practicable date won't be 2050?

Oddly, considering he says he wants to protect the Everglades, Governor Jeb Bush came out for the bill, saying it wouldn't affect federal funding or actual restoration. Even Florida's Republican U.S. Representatives had disagreed, calling on Bush to reject the bill, but to no avail. Governor Bush signed the extension into law, while claiming, "We are committed like never before to restoring the Everglades." Interesting lesson he learned from his first gubernatorial race when he lost to Lawton Chiles: say one thing, do the other.

"Anyway, at least now we're making progress," Dave says. "Maybe it's not quite as fast as people want, but it took a long time to get to this spot. So, yeah, I guess when I was a younger guy, I kind of . . . well, I'm a politician now, or at least I am part-time, so I understand these things."

We quit the subject, taking off to find a place to camp. Although hundreds, if not thousands, of fishermen spill out of Clewiston on a weekend morning, it's the end of the day now and the lake appears empty. Shimmering toward the horizon, the lake appears endless in both distance and time.

As the sun eases out of sight, we beach our boat on a spoil island made from dredging the ship channel that runs east-west through the lower half of the lake. This is where we're spending the night—on a manmade island on a man-controlled lake. We unload the boat, set up our tents, and swill a beer or two.

Dave, undeterred by past failures, wades into the lake to catch a bluegill. An alligator, not nearly as big as Dave, swims by. We're a few miles from the southern shore, and I haven't been expecting alligators so far out. But then to the gator, it's not so far out. The lake is pretty much the same depth throughout—twelve feet. No difference between here and there.

I wander off to study our island. After about two minutes, I've circumnavigated it. Guano covers everything and we're sharing space with a dead man. Luckily, he's been that way for some time. A tombstone/plaque reads: "Our Good

Buddy Doc Cooms/A Legend on the Lake/1920–1998."
Next to the plaque is an overturned bucket with a small hole
cut for an entrance—a pile of food pellets scattered inside. I
glance around, feeling watched, and under some scrubby
willows a complacent-looking rabbit is looking at me.
Maybe he's a friend of Doc's.

I walk back to camp. A couple of anhinga float by.

"Now, is that an anhinga or a cormorant?" Bill asks.

"That's a straight-billed anhinga," Dave answers readily.

"How can you tell the difference?" Bill wonders. "By the
throat?"

"No. By the straight bill."

I fix dinner or I pretend to. Before heading out, I had
stopped at a bodega in Belle Glade and bought some spicy
pork, yellow rice, and tortillas. As I warm the meal, I ask
Dave, "Can I ask you something?"

"Sure." He's been patiently answering my questions all
day. He's already had to repeat himself two or three times.

"When we were first talking, maybe on the phone, you
said you've worked here for about thirty years, and you love
it, nothing's changed. Is that part right, or not?"

"Yeah, that's about right, except for the lake. It just keeps
on changing. Most people understand this, although they
ain't happy about it. I think they're even kind of irritated
when somebody does something that's not part of the natural cycle, like dumping water we're not supposed to dump,
but we don't hear from them when we hold meetings. I've
always tried to get the local guides to come in and talk about
it, but they don't do that—they just don't like public meetings. I don't know if you've ever been to one. It's kind of like
the beginning of *Superman* where all the heads are up on
giant screens. If you're a little farmer from Okeechobee,
you'd rather sit down and share a beer with somebody and

talk about what your problem is, rather than stand out in front of a hundred people who are all sitting. On top of that you don't know whether to talk to Henry Dean [current head of the SFWMD] over here or talk to the Governing Board over there. Who's in charge?

"Here's the bottom line," he says, after a short pause. "I'd keep the lake between twelve and fifteen then let lake levels recline naturally in the fall and winter, during the dry season, without a lot of reversals in them. That would allow this area to dry down. It'd get lower, lower, and lower. Wading birds and others could get in here and—"

"But then you have EAA freaking out at that point," Bill breaks in.

"Oh, yeah," Dave agrees. "Major."

"And if you don't do it, you have the environmentalists. . . ." Bill again.

"And you know, I've got attorneys from Tallahassee that come down and go to our Governing Board meetings and threaten lawsuits and all kinds of stuff every step of the way."

"Right. Ag guys, because you keep lowering . . ." Bill adds.

"Oh, yeah."

I guess I'm slow or something, but I thought that was all over—that if the Comprehensive Plan accomplished one thing, it took care of Ag's needs—that they have nothing to complain about as far as water quantity is concerned. "They're still doing that?"

"Oh, yeah. They'll always have their lobbyists."

"But I thought that because of their land subsidence they're only going to be around for how many more years? Two decades maybe? What will happen to the EAA then?" I ask. The land hasn't subsided from erosion, as you might think, but from accelerated oxidation of the muck caused by drainage. The land has literally eaten itself away.

"I don't know. That's a good question," Dave says. "That's what was left out of the restoration plan. They could have worked out an agreement like, okay, you get your water levels that you need, right now, while you're still farming it, but when you're no longer farming it you can give the government first choice instead of selling it to development. They could have done something like that but they didn't. I'd hate to have houses out there though. Then you'd really have flood control issues."

As this yellowed full moon rises out of the east, casting a highway of sparkle across the deserted lake, I really wish they would all just shut up—not Dave and Bill but all these monomaniacal humans who just keep pushing and pushing and pushing. Since Florida became a state, all it's been is "What's in it for me?" I know this is our modern-day mantra, but in Florida it's gone beyond a mantra—it's the whole religion. And the place is peopled with zealots who are blinded by their bigotry and distrust of everybody else. It is really getting to me, pulling me down, down into the Everglades muck.

The bright side, of course, is that a lot of muck has already subsided. I can probably find my way out.

Intermission: Swimming with the Mermaids

I AM HAVING A HARD TIME HOLDING MY BREATH UNTIL I SEE her undulating. In an instant, I forget that pesky human need for oxygen and drop my jaw in wonderment. She slips through the clear springwater like a dolphin. Her iridescent tail glistens and sparkles as she gracefully makes her way toward me, and her chest, barely covered with a slip of fabric, beckons like a Siren. The call of the mermaid is silent but mesmerizing.

We lock hands and then kick dolphin-style toward her underwater castle.

Our movements are as one, and I feel as if I belong in her underwater domain. I look over at her red hair trailing elegantly behind us. She smiles and a playful bubble drifts between us.

The castle is so close. But then my lungs begin to burn, my arms grow heavier, and I find myself thrashing toward the surface.

I am not going to make it to the castle. She rises beside me.

"Hey, that was pretty good," Beth, my mermaid, soothes me. "I needed to come up, too."

I beam, not only because I can breathe again. With Beth's praise, I am well on my way to becoming a merman.

Needing a break, I've gone back to Weeki Wachee Springs—that last bastion of American mermaidhood. For more than fifty years, ever since Newton Perry, an ex-Navy frogman, put on the first underwater show here in 1947, Weeki Wachee Springs in the town of Weeki Wachee, Florida, has been a resistible roadside attraction. Over the years it has attempted to become a mermaid theme park with its water slides and riverboat cruises, a natural education center, and even an "event destination" for conventioneers, but in its simple, tacky heart, it's really just a goofy bit of fluff on the side of the highway. A lovely, mesmerizing sideshow, but a sideshow nonetheless—one of those thousands of places like naturally formed caverns, themed miniature golf courses, go-cart interchanges, model dinosaur parks, and the grab-bag of attractions with inscrutable names like the Corn Palace and the Mystery Hole that America began producing in the age of interconnected roadways and automobiles, from coast to coast, and which ensure that ours is a country of endless entertainment and fun. Fleeting, temporary havens for the weary travelers who still have hundreds of miles to go to get to their true vacation spot or next sales convention. They're a lifesaving sip of something cold and sweet on a sultry afternoon. We may scoff at them, when we're sitting in our air-conditioned homes with our fingers, gripped around the remote, on the pulse of the nation, but when we really need them, there they are with open arms.

As Weeki Wachee's general manager puts it, "People aren't aiming for here. They're usually on there way to Busch Gardens, Tarpon Springs, or the Gulf's Gold Coast."

But Weeki Wachee is my destination, a frosty sip of Coca-Cola in the heat of Everglades politics. The mermaids—those lovely, agile creatures, imprinted upon our psyche by both lore and Disney—will help me sort things out. I just know it.

Although I've never wanted to become a mer*maid*, I have always dreamed of being mer*something*, like Aquaman, calling on my fellow sea creatures to attack the bad guys and occasionally, when the need arises, riding in on my trusted sea-steed to save the day. As this fantasy became less and less likely, I dreamed of other ways to make my living in the water. I was a competitive swimmer for eighteen years. Maybe someday, I always thought, I could be a lifeguard or, like Mark Spitz, play a dentist on a Bob Hope TV special. Now, I'll gladly settle for becoming a Weeki Wachee merman.

I've arrived at Weeki Wachee feeling more than a little out of my league. It's a bit like stepping into an Elvis Presley movie. The mermaids are referred to as "girls" by their bosses. Elvis himself is piped in a continuous loop over the park's sound system; the chipping, plaster mer-statues lining the entrance to the park seem straight from a B-movie set and the Mermaid Museum, adorned with pictures of Elvis posing with assorted mermaids, informs us that the King visited Weeki Wachee twice while shooting a movie nearby. You half expect to see Him at any moment. Adding to my anxiety is the fact that although I know the mermaids use air hoses to supplement their breath-holding, my wife was informed that to be a Weeki Wachee mermaid you have to be able to hold your breath for three minutes. My anxiety isn't eased any when I talk with Gina Stremplewski, twenty-seven, and Derek Brunnet, twenty-four, both full-time performers, about their work. Derek loves his job and loves performing on any stage—underwater or above—but he reveals one ugly truth: "Everyone likes the mermaids more. They love the tail." Since the main show for the past few years has been *The Little Mermaid,* the only role for men is the part of the rescued Prince. And mermen don't wear tails in Weeki Wachee's version.

"It's a lot more hard work than you might think, but it's fun to say you're a mermaid. Not very many people can say that," Gina points out. "The only bad part is the cold. You start to get the shakes after a half hour or so." The Weeki Wachee mermaids are in the water for just a little bit longer than a half hour for each twice-daily show.

My discomfort is not eased much when I meet with Beth, the mermaid supervisor and a ten-year veteran. Beth will be judging me during my audition. I will have to hold my breath for thirty seconds (not three minutes), dive down to the bottom of the stage area, about sixteen feet deep, although the spring itself has been explored to 150 feet and goes much deeper than that through narrow openings, then swim a hundred feet underwater toward the castle, swim back on top of the water, approach the viewing window underwater and smile and wave, plus perform two deceptively simple-looking moves called the dolphin and the pinwheel.

"I love the auditions. It's real pretty when people swim up to the window and try to smile," Beth says just a bit sadistically. "But don't worry. The skills we want you to show aren't much. We can teach anybody to do what we do if you're not afraid of the water. The hardest thing beyond

getting used to the air hose is staying neutrally buoyant."
The performers release just enough air to keep them at viewing level for the underwater theater, which sits behind a
fifty-foot-wide screen of Plexiglas. The tendency for anybody in this situation who is neither a real mermaid nor a
trained one is to suck in as much air as possible, causing one
to float out of viewing range. "If I have a girl who keeps
coming to the surface, I'll give her an extra twenty minutes
in the water and she'll learn quickly. . . . Have you been in
yet? Very cold after twenty minutes. You'll see."

If I were to pass the audition, I would be hired as a trainee.
Then after eight months, I'd take a test to become a swimmer.
After about a year I'd have to take another test to become a
full-fledged mermaid, er, man. Each new level would provide
an increase in pay, and if I became a full-time mermaid, I
would get benefits, including dental, always a plus for someone who's used to being self-employed. It didn't sound so
bad except the part about the cold. I have bad circulation
in my feet and they go numb in seventy-five-degree water.
Weeki Wachee spring, percolating up through that ever-
present limestone, emerges at a constant seventy-four
degrees.

Management, either humoring me or prepared to be
humored by me, is treating my audition as if it's the real
thing. Beth will be hidden in the cramped operations' center
on the other side of the viewing screen with a score sheet to
grade my performance.

Out on the rock that looks over the underwater theater,
dressed in not-so-sexy surfer trunks, I'm wishing I had
pumped iron—if not for the last five years, then at least the
past month. Ready or not, though, I begin my tryout and
dive toward the middle of the pool. As casually as possible,

I undulate toward a stage prop, an anchor made of plywood that's used to symbolize the Prince's ship in *The Little Mermaid*.

The anchor is lowered about five feet underwater so I'll have something to grab ahold of. Grabbing a last breath, I go down with it, wondering, for the first time, why I'm doing this.

Weeki Wachee has an underwater sound system with powerful speakers that allow the mermaids to hear both the audience and Beth in the control booth. It's impossible to see the audience through the vinyl windows without goggles or a face mask, so being able to hear their appreciation is the performers' only reward. Today, my reward is laughter. I suddenly realize I'm doing a good Dizzy Gillespie imitation with my puffed-out cheeks and bulging eyes. Wanting to look suave and sophisticated, I deflate my cheeks and don't even make it thirty seconds. Damn.

Then, in succession, I tread water, swim underwater the length of the spring, and sprint freestyle on the way back. (I contemplate doing butterfly to make up for my poor show-ing on the breath-holding test and make a mental note to remind Beth I swam on my college team.)

Then comes the hard part—the dolphin and pinwheel moves. The dolphin consists of gracefully arching one's back while spinning backward in a fluid full circle while maintaining pointed toes—not to mention a semblance of dignity. It's then that I finally realize the tables have been turned all morning. Instead of my spoofing Weeki Wachee, Weeki Wachee is spoofing me. When has a guy ever had to point his toes underwater? There's a reason guys don't do synchronized swimming: We'd look stupid. But some kind of can-do attitude overwhelms the logic of simply climbing out of the water, and I face my audience refusing to give up.

The dolphin is so far beyond me that I come up choking two or three times before I complete a full circle, looking more like an octopus caught in a whirlpool than a graceful man-fish. I keep trying, but after my twentieth attempt, I hear Beth, with bellyaching laughter in the background, suggest I try approaching the window for my smile and wave. Uncharitably, I'm hoping the laugher will bust a gut.

Beth has warned me about a cocky guy who swam face-first into the window, so I gingerly make my way forward. I stop a few inches short, vainly gather my composure, and then smile and wave simultaneously. To understand how this felt, simply remember how you feel in those dreams you have of finding yourself in school, dressed in only your underwear. Jacobs, the theme park manager, has apparently been beside Beth the entire time, for all of a sudden he's coaching me via the underwater speaker, "Bigger smile. Bigger smile. That's it. Now wave. Wave." By this point, although I oblige him, I know for certain they're having fun with me. My realization is confirmed when Beth comes swimming out to me in her mermaid tail and bikini top and blurts out, "Felt like a dork, huh?"

It doesn't matter, though, because something's worked. I feel refreshed, almost carefree—nothing like really making a fool of yourself to force you to let go. That's when we swim off together, hand in hand, headed for the Little Mermaid's castle under the sea. With Beth's tail on, just for a second and maybe because I've held my breath for a tad too long, I feel like I'm holding hands with a real live mermaid. Only I am wishing Beth is a manatee and that the crystal-clear waters of Weeki Wachee would flow into a briny, unpolluted Gulf of Mexico, joining together to nurture the Everglades—something to confirm, just like in that Jimmy Cliff song, that everything is gonna be all right.

Something About Sugar

HEADING SOUTH, LET'S TURN OUR ATTENTION TOWARD the sugar problem.

In 1800 sugar accounted for less than 1 percent of our daily caloric intake. Today, it accounts for 20 percent; the average American consumes 160 pounds of sugar each year when you include liquid sugars, such as high-fructose corn syrup.

At the going rate, each of us will be eating 200 pounds of sugar annually by 2010.

Ever tried to quit sugar? Go on the Atkins Diet, perhaps? My best effort was twenty-seven hours. In the beginning, while talking to somebody on the phone or spacing out, I would eat something as innocuous as a slice of bread, only later learning the bread was made with sugar. Another time

I absentmindedly made my regular coffee, which includes a spoonful of sugar. I couldn't eat out because restaurants add sugar to everything—from steak to broccoli in clandestine marinades and not-so-secret sauces. The time I made it twenty-seven hours, it was no accident when I finally slipped—it was an all-out frantic intake of anything sweet and fatty. I ate half a pan of my children's Rice Krispies Treats as they stared at me, tears rolling down their grubby, sugar-stained faces.

Like most people, I like sugar, but I love sugarcane. It's my personal nectar. When I was a young boy, my mom would find some farmer selling stalks of cane alongside the highway in Louisiana. She loved things like this—rich, sustaining tastes straight from the earth. We'd cut the stalk at each joint and then peel the armor-like outer husk off. Inside, a substance that looked like a hundred wet straws tightly bound together waited for me to bite down onto it. You chewed on this, and the sweet juice flooded your mouth. Then, when the juice was all gone, you got to spit out the residue, called the bagasse, without anyone getting mad at your bad manners.

Many adults seem unimpressed by the juice's charms—too many years of the refined stuff, I guess. But to a kid, it's the goods. Recently, I bought a few stalks at our local grocery store in Maine (imagine what those early sugarcane boosters would think of that). We juiced it in our electric juicer, tried to make paper out of the bagasse, and dried it into sticky syrup interspersed with crystals. My children loved the crystally molasses but merely tolerated the pure squeezed juice, much preferring sucking it out of the inner stalk to drinking it out of a glass. I drank a cup before swimming at the Y and had a great workout. Unrefined, cane juice is full of complex carbohydrates and is an excellent energy source—much longer lasting than refined sugar.

What's my point? I don't have a problem with sugar; in fact, I'm even a defender. The National Academy of Sciences recently released a report that we could receive up to 25 percent of our calories from sugar and still be eating healthfully. So, unlike a lot of people, I'm not against sugar or sugarcane; I just don't think it should be cultivated in the Everglades.

Some sugarcane, specifically *Saccharum giganteum*, is actually native to the American Southeast, including Florida. Its woolly plumes swayed through the sultry air long before Friends of the Everglades declared war on Big Sugar, a general usage term for the sugar industry. In a way, therefore, sugar does belong in South Florida.

Saccharum giganteum only produces a modicum of sucrose when compared to *Saccharum officinarum*, the sugarcane sanctioned and coveted by pirates, priests, capitalist defilers, slave owners, and others for hundreds of years. *Saccharum officinarum* means noble sugar, and what a noble plant it is! The lust for sugar and its ever-increasing value to the world market directly led to the American slave trade and even sparked the American Revolution.

Remember "Salutary Neglect" from your high school or college American history class? It refers to the Brits' neglect of the American colonies from the early 1600s to the mid-1700s—a neglect that directly led to the colonists' sense of independence. During this period, the colonists established a lucrative triangular trade that had nothing to do with England. Ships from New England sailed first to Africa, exchanging New England rum for slaves. The slaves went from Africa to the Caribbean. In the Caribbean the ships exchanged slaves for molasses. Then the ships returned to

New England, where the molasses was used to make rum and sugar.

Thanks to the debts created by its wars with France, England instituted a new policy toward the colonies in the 1760s in an attempt to tax them back into line. They tried to enforce an earlier act, the Molasses Act of 1733, which taxed all molasses, rum, and sugar that the colonies imported from countries other than Britain and her colonies, by establishing the Writs of Assistance in 1760. The said writs allowed British officials to search any home or store that was suspected of harboring smuggled goods. This was followed by ever more oppressive taxes, including the Sugar Act in 1764. "An act . . . for altering and disallowing several drawbacks on exports from this kingdom, and more effectually preventing the clandestine conveyance of goods to and from the said colonies and plantation, and improving and securing the trade between the same and Great Britain. Whereas it is expedient that new provisions and regulations should be established for improving the revenue of this kingdom, and for extending and securing the navigation and commerce between Great Britain and your Majesty's dominions in America . . . there shall be raised, levied, collected, and paid, unto his Majesty, his heirs and successors, for and upon all white or clayed sugars of the produce or manufacture of any colony or plantation in America, not under the dominion of his Majesty . . . which shall be imported or brought into any colony or plantation in America, which now is, or hereafter may be, under the dominion of his Majesty, his heirs and successors, the several rates and duties following . . ."

Understandably, it took the colonists a while to revolt after this tax was enacted, considering how impossible it is to get through, but revolt they did. You think the Boston Tea

Party was about tea? It was all about molasses, sugar, and rum. Tea was just one of the many commodities being taxed under the Sugar Act and was expendable. Which would you rather toss into the sea—molasses and sugar that could be used for making rum and money, or a few barrels of tea?

Anyway, back to *Saccharum*. It is believed to have originated in New Guinea and was cultivated there for thousands of years before anyone north and west of India new there was something sweeter than Tupelo honey. At first the New Guineans grew it as feed for their pigs, but over time, the pigs lost out and the New Guineans grew it for themselves. Just imagine, you're out on the hunt when you lose your spear. The leopard, originally the hunted, is now the hunter. You're scared. You're weak. You're crying for your momma. What do you do? Curl up and pray the carnivorous cat doesn't like pretend-dead meat? Feed some sugarcane to your trusty pig, let him off his leash, and may the best animal win? No, no. Instead, you reach into the bulging pouch at your side and pop that life-giving cane into your own mouth! And since this is not the refined crap we eat today, you get a boost of energy allowing you the strength of five of your normal self. Still being a coward, said boost merely sweeps you back to your village where you cower behind your wife's sturdy legs until she's speared the leopard just as it leaps over your thatched sugarcane wall. She, of course, being smarter and sturdier, has been chewing on the cane for years. Word of your discovery spreads, and soon everybody wants some.

After that, cultivation of *Saccharum* spans Asia. The Polynesian sailors take sugarcane with them wherever they go, which is practically everywhere, and while their balls swing in the Pacific swells, telling them which way to go, they munch on sugarcane for energy and hydration. In

China and India it is boiled down into a syrup, made into the first crystallized sugar, and used as a medicine as well as a sweetener. The Mediterraneans find out about it in 500 B.C. when the Persian King Darius marches into the Indus Valley and discovers reeds that produce honey without bees. Darius is a good warrior but perhaps not so sharp when it comes to making money—apparently he leaves without taking any cane. Alexander the Great, the great marketer that he is, does have one of his generals bring sugar to his people a little later in history. And that's when sugar begins to break its Asian confines. Relatively soon afterward, the Arabs beat the sugar recipe out of the Persians. When they take over Spain, they bring sugar with them (perhaps it's what they eat while on the march). Whatever the case, they grow sugarcane in Valencia and sell sugar to the merchants of Venice, who market it as a priceless medicine. Everybody loves sugar but lacking supply, demand doesn't really increase. Over time, though, the Iberians plant sugarcane wherever it will grow and import African slaves for the dirty work—the tilling, planting, harvesting, and pressing.

Eventually Columbus makes his second trip to Hispaniola (today's island of the Dominican Republic and Haiti) and plants the very first *Saccharum* in the New World. On successive trips, the Spaniards even bring some to Florida, planting it between getting their butts kicked by those local Floridians already mentioned, the Calusa. Thanks to the Calusa and the Everglades itself, the sugarcane industry doesn't really flourish in Florida during this time, but it does elsewhere throughout Spanish America.

The Dutch take over Brazil along with its local sugar industry in the early 1600s. When the Portuguese kick them out of Brazil, they move to the Caribbean Islands, teaching this science to the Brits in the Barbados, who then switch from tobacco to sugarcane, with the help of slaves sold to them by . . . can you guess? . . . the Dutch. And that's about when all that slave-molasses-sugar-rum stuff starts that eggs on the American Revolution.

As mentioned, because of a certain "swamp," sugarcane cultivation doesn't really take off in Florida as it does in the Caribbean and Louisiana. However, after disease wipes out the Calusa and the Seminole Wars decimate the few Indians living in and around the Everglades and finally the semi-successful damming/drainage/levee efforts in the early part of the twentieth century dry things up a bit, humans once again attempt to grow sugarcane in Florida on a large scale, just below Lake Okeechobee.

This drained land is billed as the richest soil in the world. Anything can grow there because the peat is so rich from all those years of flooding and burn-offs. Hell, even sugarcane—a tropical species—could probably grow there. And so the little farmers move in, clearing the land at an acre a week where elders and custard apple grow or even worse, an acre every two months where saw grass reigns. They have to clear the land by hand because farm equipment will not work in the muck. As they pull up roots and chop down saw grass, they light fires that inevitably grow out of control because the land itself—the dense muck—catches fire, too. The sun beats down on them. Mosquitoes attack. Entire families die—wasting away into the now-turbid waters, beaten by exhaustion, malaria, and dismay. This isn't the paradise they've bought into. Depending on their birthplace, they long for the boredom of an Ohio corn farm or the poverty and embarrassment of a failed business back in sweet old Georgia. Oh, what they would give for a Georgia peach.

The worst is yet to come. The truck farmers, the people

hoping to grow summer vegetables and fruits in Florida's winter and truck them north, holler with joy as their newly planted crops burst above the soil, growing faster than anything they've ever seen, but after a few days the plants turn a sickly yellow and just slowly die—the acclaimed rich soils of the reclaimed Everglades aren't so rich after all. They hold no trace elements, and so the crops starve to death.

After they have spent all their time and money on getting their sugarcane started—or corn or beans or whatever they are originally trying to get rich on—the stuff simply won't grow, or if it does, the yield is nothing to brag about. Imagine that, a crop, dependent on extremely dry land with a water table two feet below the surface and desirous of constant, hot tropical temperatures, won't grow in a mostly temperate wetland! Never mind that the Florida legislature and its proxies, realtors, and land developers have promoted the land as perfect for sugarcane and other consumables, all the while backing scientists who claim the land will never need fertilization. It's gonna grow because, hell, look at all that decayed vegetable matter lying there, waiting for some enterprising young man to reap his fortune. Any fool could grow something in that!

Eventually, as farmers use fertilizers and pesticides to save their crops, the farmland improves. Thousands of people have bought the ten-acre lots being sold by the railroad companies and the State of Florida. A few hundred of these landowners go out and try to farm their property. A score or two succeed.

Meanwhile, this land, which has been conceived of and sold as a poor man's paradise—hundreds of thousands of acres broken up into ten-acre lots worked by people making a simple living—is for the most part abandoned, either never worked or when worked and failed, simply left behind encumbered with back taxes and unpaid loans. It is up for the taking, a huge piece of stinky-sweet cheese simply waiting for some big rat to come along and gobble it up. And that's what happens.

A series of individuals, a co-op, and even a few companies attempt to jump-start the sugar industry just below Lake Okeechobee starting with four thousand acres, but successively each fails. Then, in 1925, Bror Dahlberg seizes control of the Everglades Agricultural Area, staking it out as sugar country once and for all. Dahlberg takes over where others have faltered and turns the original four thousand acres into a hundred thousand, all to the south and west of Lake Okeechobee. Dahlberg's firm, the Southern Sugar Company, stutters, just like the others, and in 1931 C. S. Mott, a shareholder in Dahlberg's company, buys all of Dahlberg's holdings. Mott, a former GM chairman, renames the enterprise United States Sugar, and an empire is born.

In the 1930s U.S. Sugar and other sugar farmers come up with a novel approach for their labor: de facto slavery. Although noble sugarcane will not grow productively in the EAA, cross-breeding has developed a cane suitable for the areas' soil and environment and U.S. Sugar is soon producing more than 80 percent of Florida's sugar crop. It is still backbreakingly difficult to grow and harvest. Except during the Depression, whites won't do the work, and after a while local blacks won't, either, or can't, simply knowing what's what. For a while, the companies import black workers from all over the South, with promises of cash payment, a place to stay, and the warmth of Florida. What the farmers haven't explained is that the workers will never see any of that cash. They will work for six excruciating months without a single dollar touching their bleeding hands—because they're charged for things like transportation to the work site from

Alabama, training, board, harvesting tools, and even ID badges. Money is advanced to the workers for these items so the workers start off in debt. From there on it is a losing battle, since the most they can ever make in a day is $3. They usually don't get this $3 a day for the first couple of weeks anyway, since this is the training period, and so the typical worker stays in debt the entire time. (A similar thing goes on today for migrant pickers in Florida's citrus fields.)

As a result of these unconscionable labor practices, U.S. Sugar does well in the 1930s, becoming one of Florida's richest companies. Also, as a result of these very same labor practices, the federal government indicts U.S. Sugar for peonage and illegal beatings of its workers, accusing U.S. Sugar of violating the right and privilege of ". . . citizens to be free from slavery." Although the case against U.S. Sugar is strong, the federal court judge, Fred Barker, a local needless-to-say white, knows what's healthy for him. He dismisses all charges on the grounds that the grand jury has been improperly impaneled.

Still, U.S. Sugar falters a bit during the war, as every sugar grower and producer does across the world, because the price of sugar plummets to $4 a pound. But, lest anyone forget, these guys are rascals. Although they stop abusing American laborers, it isn't out of a reformed conscience but because the U.S. government once again comes to sugar's rescue, providing new slaves, er, workers, by allowing Bahamians and Jamaicans to be "imported" to work American fields. On account of the war, staggering unemployment in the Caribbean makes cutting American cane seem better than a day spent hanging out starving in the sun.

At first things go pretty well for the new cane cutters. The U.S. government provides the contracts and pays for the workers' round-trip travel. The contracts guarantee the workers thirty cents an hour, plus housing and medical care. The good times last a little past the war until 1947, when American men returned for good from the war to the workforce. That's when the government bows out of the human import-export business, although still allowing sugar farmers to hire temporary workers from Jamaica, mostly because U.S. citizens still won't work for Big Sugar. The extant policy toward migrant labor in the sugar industry becomes institutionalized with the 1952 Immigration and Nationality Act that defines temporary nonimmigrant workers and makes it possible for businesses and farmers to continue to hire such workers.

After 1952 things just get better and better for the sugar barons. The Corps perfects its water management, keeping water in Okeechobee for the farmers to draw from but draining enough of it to keep the water table two feet below the surface. Meanwhile, the soil grows richer as fertilization techniques improve. And new breeds of sugarcane are developed quickly enough to stay ahead of ever-adapting pests and disease.

By 1960 the sugar companies, although their holdings are much vaster, only farm roughly fifty thousand acres of cane. Vegetables and fruits cover seventy thousand; cattle use roughly another fifty thousand. The other four hundred thousand acres in the Everglades Agricultural Area remain undeveloped.

Then 1961 comes around and Castro gets our attention. The EAA is never again the same. Kennedy's paranoia makes its way to the cane fields decidedly faster than Khrushchev's bombs. Cuba has not only been the world's largest producer of sugar but also America's main supplier. With the new American embargo, Cuban sugar can no longer be imported. America's sugar growers will have to save the day!

The United States places a tariff on all foreign sugar and creates a price-support system for domestic sugar that becomes known as the Sugar Program—a program so sweet that only a diabetic would pass it up. Meanwhile, the government hands out quotas to favored nations to provide America with sugar, knowing full well that Florida and the other sugar-producing states can't fill the Cuban void.

Not surprisingly, the sugar companies dump the vegetables, kill the cattle, and plant more cane.

Today, sugarcane sways over some 440,000 acres. In Florida alone it's a multibillion-dollar-a-year industry, employing 40,000 people. The enslaved cane cutters are gone, thanks to improved mechanical harvesters and endless lawsuits on the cane cutters' behalf, but the sugar industry is still reviled as the Darth Vader of the Everglades by environmentalists.

If it weren't for the sugar plantations, the EAA would still be the Everglades (right, and the citrus growers wouldn't have gobbled the land up for themselves). If it weren't for the sugarcane farming runoff, the water would still be pure enough for saw grass in the water conservation areas just below the farms. If it weren't for the power of the sugar companies over the politicians, the Corps and the SFWMD wouldn't be wasting its time on testing and then building 330 Aquifer Storage and Recovery systems. Perhaps, if it weren't for the sugar growers, Senator Bob Graham (who's received more than $100,000 from sugar companies and their proxies over the course of his senatorial career) would have made sure the Comprehensive Everglades Restoration Plan focused more on the Everglades and less on providing water for Florida's burgeoning population and indomitable sugar farmers.

So sugar farming is in a pass-the-buck kind of way responsible for slavery, both actual slavery and the de facto kind mentioned earlier. So it's helped kill the Everglades. So it still stands in the way, and no matter what the Corps does to help the Everglades, the old natural flow cannot be returned to the Everglades as long as those farms stay put.

But still, is sugar really all that bad?

I contact a friend whose family farmed cotton not far from my hometown in Mississippi and who's recently worked as a lobbyist in D.C. for the sugar industry. My plan: have him find a farmer to talk with me, show me his farm, so I can get the farmer's side of the story. He finds Russell Kilpatrick, a sugarcane farmer working a few thousand acres just west of southern Lake Okeechobee.

"I'm still looking for my damn check," Russell says with a half smile. He looks a bit like the sheriff on *The Dukes of Hazard* and reminds me of farmers I knew growing up in Mississippi. He is both serious and joking at the same time.

"You don't get a subsidy for growing sugar?" I ask. Standing outside his office, on the edge of his two-thousand-acre sugarcane farm, I've just told him most people think sugar farmers live off the government.

He looks at me carefully—the same kind of look I got back at Weeki Wachee. "No. There's no subsidy for sugar-cane farming." But what about all the articles, the ranting of the environmentalists? "They're full of shit." He laughs pretty hard. After that, we hop into his pickup and drive toward the cane fields.

We pull over next to an elephantine cane chopper that is cutting the stalks near their bottom, feeding them to a thresher that sheds them of any remaining leaves and then tosses the canes into a large bed in back. It takes one man driving this machine to cut what it used to take four workers to cut manually; the harvester cuts and loads nearly forty tons in a day. Here, Russell explains the sugar program in a way I can finally understand.

"Some American farmers are subsidized, like the peanut growers. The way the sugar program works, though, is like this: I'll cut all this cane. It's got to be at the mill by midnight Sunday. By Thursday they know how many pounds of sugar my crop's going to make. I can then take out a government loan at eighteen cents a pound on this sugar. There's interest on that and it's fairly high. It ain't a freebie. But they'll loan you eighteen cents a pound on 80 percent of your crop. They'll cut you a check that day. Now, the hell of it is, the way sugar is sold, whether or not you take that loan, your sugar goes into a warehouse at U.S. Sugar. Whatever my share is of what's in the warehouse—whether it's 10 percent or 2 percent—I get paid by the month, as they sell the entire warehouse of sugar. It takes twelve to fourteen months to sell all that sugar. My money's tied up for a year either way, but I've taken some of those loans. When cane only averaged eighteen cents a pound, I lived off of my helicopter service." (Russell sidelines as a helicopter pilot.)

I'm still not quite seeing why this is so bad, being paid a guaranteed eighteen cents a pound. "So eighteen cents a pound is a bad loan?"

"No, no, no, I mean we only got eighteen cents a pound out of sugar the year before last. All year. The whole year. Some of it sold at sixteen. And the best I can figure it, it's costing me nineteen cents a pound to grow it. So we was actually in the red even though I'd taken that loan."

"Right now, it's still costing you nineteen cents a pound to grow?"

"Yeah, right around that, maybe twenty. Changes according to the grower."

"So, say you take that eighteen-cent loan and then you pay them back, when?"

"The way that works, say they start selling sugar and my part comes out. The government comes first. They get their money back before I get any of mine. Right now it's running about twenty cents."

"And that's what people are calling a subsidy?" I ask.

"Yep."

In the strict definition of the word *subsidy*, despite Russell's protestations, the Sugar Program mostly fits the definition: "Monetary assistance granted by a government to a person or a private commercial enterprise." But looking at it from Russell's perspective, I'd have to agree: The Sugar Program is not much of a handout for the small-scale sugar farmers; it's a handout for the sugar manufacturers. If the sugar corporations—in Florida this means U.S. Sugar based in Clewiston, and Florida Crystals based in West Palm Beach—actually bought the cane from the farmers (and being billion-dollar companies, they could do it), then there wouldn't be any need for the government to intercede by providing the low-interest loans. But since that isn't the case, the big sugar companies get to acquire the sugarcane without having to pay anything, until they actually sell the sugar they make from the farmers' cane. In other words, the sugar companies get the materials for their product for free until they sell their product. Imagine if we all had it that good.

That's where the political payoffs and hanky-panky come into play. The sugar industry spends millions of dollars a year on lobbying, and they contribute amply to state and national campaigns. Looking at the tariffs that keep sugar around twenty cents a pound in the United States and the sugar companies indomitably in Florida, I'd say their efforts pay off big time. Before you start boycotting American sugar, however, understand that every developed nation in the world, except for Australia, has a sugar subsidy/tariff program that makes other farmers wilt with envy.

The vast majority of the sugar farms are not owned by people like Russell Kilpatrick. Florida Crystals and U.S. Sugar own 90 percent of the sugarcane land in Florida. So these companies make it on both ends, as growers and as sellers of the refined product. As a result of the tariff and the price government pays for sugar, Florida Crystals and U.S. Sugar make an extra $50–100 million or so every year. Meanwhile, it's estimated that we, the consumers, pay an extra $1.9 billion a year for products made with sugar— based on the idea that the tariffs are adding $1.9 billion to sugar and the products made with sugar, since the world price for sugar is half of the United States' set price.

Now, one might make the argument that we, the consumers of sugar, could and should do something about this. Sugar, many believe, has no nutritional value beyond simple carbohydrates, which when used by the body merely give us a fleeting amount of energy—like just enough *oomph* to get off the couch and grab a bag of sweetened corn chips (yep, read the label). Sugar helps make us fat and ruins our teeth. We all know this yet we keep spooning it in. Why? Because it's a drug. Sugar, like heroin and other drugs, releases endorphins in the brain that please us. This is why we crave the stuff and continually prefer foods with higher sugar content. And all of this—the government incentives, the profits, the druglike appeal, the horticultural science, the political bribery, the honest hard work of people like Russell Kilpatrick—is why the sugar farms block any chance for the Everglades ever to be restored.

But let's get back to Russell working his ass off on his farm.

"But let's face it," Russell says, "when sugar went to sixteen cents a pound, you didn't see the price of Coca-Cola go down, you didn't see candy bars lower in price; in fact, the price of candy bars actually went up. Sugar in the store didn't get cheaper. Some damn body is making a hell of a pile of money, and it isn't us."

"How are you going to make this work? It's costing you nineteen cents a pound to grow?"

"Well, I'll tell you what, in the eighties sugar was bringing almost twenty-two to twenty-three cents, for years. That's one reason we decided to go from cattle to cane. Also, NAFTA killed us. I never thought my dad'd get out of the cattle business, but he just said the hell with it. Sugar looked too good."

Russell's driving me around his farm. Every once in a while we hop out to inspect a truck or have him show me something up close. We stop beside an irrigation ditch.

"What is that plant?" I ask, pointing to some green debris clogging his little canal.

"That is water hyacinth—just another one of them damn things that I've got to get around and spray or take a backhoe and clean out."

"What do you use mostly, poison or a backhoe?"

"A little bit of both."

This reminds me of all the work the SFWMD does to keep its canals flowing freely so they can continue to dump that 1.7 billion gallons of water a day into the ocean. All day long they have boats scouring the canals clean, ripping out water plants that might impede the water's flow. It costs $70 million a year to maintain the South Florida canal system.

Russell says, "I was talking to a guy at Sugar this morning. The District's dumping a massive amount of water into the ocean right now. Just opening it up. The hell of it is, they did that last year and they really put us in a bad pickle. We ran out of irrigation water. I could not get any irrigation water out of the place because there was a bad drought, but they turned three foot of water out just at the start of the drought."

"They did?"

"Yes, sir."

"Did they think some big storm was coming?"

"No, hell no. They listened to these fishermen."

"Oh, it was the fisherman?"

"Hell, yeah. The lake's on a ten-year cycle anyway. Ten, twelve years, we have our ten-foot lakes, and Water Management admitted they knew this drought was coming. And they dropped it anyway and turned it all out, flushed the brackish water out of the Fort Myers area, killing millions of fish. Them people were raising hell. And then there we were, without any water."

We're driving again and he slams on the brakes, pointing to some cane.

"Some of this here looks kind of yucky. This is all take-out cane."

"What's that mean? The other kind is called what cane? The one they were harvesting back there, what is that called?"

"That is plant cane, I just planted. That is first harvest after planting and that's always usually your better harvest. This take-out cane is some of the first I've planted. It's been cut five times. After four or five times you take it out and replant. I'll go in with some Roundup, spray over it. It kills the cane, the grass, the weeds, and I'll come back and spray it one more time to make sure, and then at end of the summer I'll start disking."

"So you don't let it sit for a whole year then or plant something to help the soil?"

"No, I'd lose a crop. Can't afford to do that." We're driving again. We've almost circled half the property when he stops by a large pond. "This is the end side of a retention pond. There's a hundred acres here."

"Whoa. And that's what they're telling you to do? Set aside a hundred acres on your own land to clean the water?"

"Yup. Let me ask you this. Do you know where phosphorus comes from?"

Your runoff, I try.

"Phosphorus is a natural metal in the soil. You go toward Tampa and all up there, there's big old mines and that's where it comes from. There's natural phosphorus in the Everglades. Them guys don't want to talk about that."

This new retention pond will filter the phosphorus and nitrogen out of his runoff. It's construction was mandated by the Everglades Forever Act, under something called Best Management guidelines developed by the state.

"I was sitting at this damn meeting one day and these goddamned guys, it took them five minutes to introduce these people, how many Ph.D.s and this and that and dummy me sitting up there. I said I ain't got no Ph.D.s. Nothing but hard luck and hard work, but all I'm hearing is fertilizer this and fertilizer that. I just want to let you guys know that I don't use phosphorus in my fertilizer. It's already in the ground. Why buy something you don't need?"

"So you don't use any phosphorus in your fertilizer then?"

189

"Well, very seldom. I'm going to say I've got a couple fields that I guess I had to put a little bit into, but it's something I don't do every year."

"And you've got some fields where you don't need it at all?"

"Probably 90 percent. Like I told them, you put what nitrogen and what phosphorus you need. You don't go out there and go crazy. Fertilizer costs a lot of money. And the other thing, phosphorus cuts down on the sugar content. Some vegetables like phosphorus, but sugarcane does not."

We're on the other side of his retention pond now.

"Now, here's one of the pump stations," Russell says. "I've got the pump set in. I still got to build the pump house around it."

Trying to see if I've got an understanding of the Best Management guidelines Russell is working under, I point to the pump and then to the retention pond. "So this is what will happen. Your runoff—you'll pump out into that."

"Right."

"And then where will that water get pumped to?"

"Well, it won't be getting pumped. It will gravity drain. It gets so high then it starts spilling out.

"Into what?"

"Same place it's going now—into the river," he says, looking exasperated. "These Best Management practices are simple, but they're more than exceeding what standards or goals they were given. You see, phosphorus settles because it's heavy. The water that flows out of this pond will be mostly free of phosphorus."

Russell explains how on another farm, they're reusing the settled phosphorus on areas that are low in phosphorus and even admits that the Best Management guidelines made people think. "It urged people on to doing something that might end up improving yields."

"All of these Best Management improvements—they're going to cost you a million dollars," I say, sensing that Russell is being too generous on my account. That's the figure he's given me earlier for the mandatory improvements. "I couldn't imagine having to cough up a hundred dollars to do my work, let alone a million. Can you see any benefits in the restoration project?"

He pauses for a moment. "Well, it's definitely a pain in the ass to do all this. Here I'm going to have to be pumping water from now on when I wouldn't normally have to pump. I mean, I've got the expense of three engines sitting there—three pumps I've got to maintain and put fuel in from now on, and I've got to get up in the middle of the night and come down and check them. You can't just let them sit and run all night. Sometimes two o'clock in the morning, somebody's got to go check—"

"And that'd be you, huh?"

"It's a pain in the ass," he says, laughing, then returns to my question. "I'm for fixing things. If there is an environmental problem, do what you got to do, but look at the Audubon Society and those other damn people, the Sierra Club, look at the people who's in there. Who are they?"

"Ex-developers?" I guess.

"Yep. Old moneymakers. A lot of these people, that's where they made their money—off the land. They've got their money, but they don't want anybody else to. The only other thing I see about these folks is they would look to see a good deal on farmland so they can buy it cheap for development."

We talk about family—about Russell having learned farming from his dad and wanting to teach his son the same.

We drive past a burning field. It seems to me it might help with public relations a bit if in this day and age they were able to work their fields without creating so much pollution.

"Well, if you look in there, it's fairly clean, but if you cut it without burning, the machine just gets clogged up. All this stuff has to be burned out. All the trash that's in there, the leaves and that sort of thing." He points over to a stand that hasn't been burned. It looks impenetrable—almost as if it hasn't been planted but has sprouted naturally out of the precious muck. "Can you imagine a machine running through there? I know people get upset about all the smoke, but there's been environmental studies done and it's not a bad smoke. It's a hot fire, it goes quick."

Cane has been cultivated this way around the world for at least a thousand years, and old ways die hard. They've designed machines that can take out the stalks without burning the field first, but these machines leave everything else behind. In Russell's mind, that's just a pain in the ass because you've still got to do something with all the leavings.

He shows me a row with tiny shoots.

"I took the cows off this last June and I should have had it planted, but Dad got sick. I flew to Tampa almost daily for about seven weeks every day. Lung cancer. He was a tough old shit. I just figured if anybody could whip it, he could. . . . I helped Dad with all this. Making all we got because we didn't come up having much."

I ask him what he'd like to see happen in the future besides no more new regulations.

"I'd like to see sugar get back to twenty-three cents—where it was. It hung in the twenty-twos and twenty-threes for years. That'd be good," he says, standing outside his office now, cowboy hat in hand. "Nothing else goes down. Why can't produce stay up? Pickups, they haven't gone down a bit. And hardware? You go down to the parts store. Those prices sure haven't gone down. I needed some three-eights-by-six-inch bolts, eighteen bucks apiece. Two tin bolts, thirty-six bucks. Plus tax. Imagine that."

Through the Saw Grass

"WAKE UP, HODDING, WE'VE GOT TO GET GOING."

I'm being poked in the ribs. My tormentor, David Conover, climbs to his feet, rocking our makeshift, floating island. Without hesitation, he begins swinging his arms; he's done this all night. The combination of his swinging fetish, the incessant whine of mosquitoes a millimeter beyond my mosquito netting, and the shakiness of our sleeping platform have overwhelmed me with insomnia.

In other words I've only slept two hours or so. "Fuck off. It's not even morning yet."

Then from a few feet away, another of my companions chimes in. "If we don't find a way through today, I really think we should turn around." This is Steve Robinson, the

park naturalist. He seems to be slightly daunted, having never done what we're attempting to do: cross the Everglades from north to south through the saw grass from the Tamiami Trail to Florida Bay. He's tried cutting through from the Pahayokee Lookout once before but was stopped by a burgeoning forest of mangroves. After three days of all-out poling, covering less than half a mile per hour, we've run into the exact same brake of mangroves.

"Well, then. I say we must make an early go of it," my third companion appears to trill as she rises from beneath her mosquito netting with an ever-present smile. Saranne, the irrepressible. I've brought her along on this outing on the advice of mutual friends because she's a professional outdoorsperson. She's led Outward Bound trips for decades and has tackled adventures on every continent. But her persistently positive behavior might spell her death. I don't care how many dangers she's overcome.

The not sleeping is really getting to me.

We're attempting something that's *never* been done before—only, of course, it probably has. Everyone likes to make that claim about his or her trip through the Everglades. Like the New Orleans *Times-Democrat* 1883 expedition that faced so many difficulties on Lake Okeechobee, we're attempting to cross the Everglades from north to south. Like them, we started where the Everglades begins, but unlike for them, as we've established, that no longer means at the south end of Lake Okeechobee. No, we've started where the Everglades currently begins—at the Tamiami Trail, the dividing line between the Everglades Agricultural Area and Everglades National Park. Also, instead of attempting the sensible route and following the flow of Shark River Slough into the Gulf of Mexico, I've decided that we should go directly south and attempt to cross the shallowest water possible to see what is happening in the peripheral parts of the park. The fact that the "peripheral" part makes up the majority of the park and that the Shark River Slough still works a lot like it did historically has me intrigued. Or, I should say, *had* me intrigued. Now I just want to find a way out.

I crawl out of my sleeping bag, doing the funky chicken to chase the mosquitoes away, and jump naked into the waist-high water without a thought toward alligators, snakes, or other horrors. Such behavior would have been unthinkable three days earlier when we scouted our put-in along the Tamiami Trail, near the Shark Valley Visitor Center. There, staring at a seemingly impenetrable wall of willows and pepper plants and the endless world of saw grass beyond, I was afraid to step a few feet away from the group. How were we supposed to proceed through the thickets and saw grass, let alone survive, for a week? But on the second day, when it took more than thirty minutes to push our canoes 150 yards through some eight-foot-tall saw grass, the endless saw grass began to change from "Eerie Waterworld" to something much less horrific. Something enjoyable, even enviable, in fact. I fell face first in mazes of saw grass, inadvertently drinking the fresh, clear water (successfully vanquishing any thought of a murky, festering tropical marsh), repeatedly submerging my whole body countless times until I no longer feared the Everglades. I arose reborn, baptized by this brutalized ecosystem. Perhaps my sins weren't washed away, but this was when and where the Everglades completely, solidly became my Place—forever. John Steinbeck once wrote a depressing, inconceivably trite novel about failure called *The Winter of Our Discontent*; it was my favorite book my junior year in high school. The protagonist almost commits suicide because of his own failures, but visits to something he calls "the Place" soothe his pains enough to continue on. So now I'm wondering: What am I going to do if my Place disappears forever?

We started out on November 9, 2002, getting an Everglades City canoe outfitter to drop us off a few miles past the park's Shark Valley Visitor Center on the Tamiami Trail. Some Outward Bounders, friends of Saranne, have shown us this put-in, though calling it a put-in is a bit of a stretch. It's a truncated, abandoned road running parallel to and south of a portion of the Tamiami Trail.

It's a desolate spot, made even more so when I walk a half mile out from our launching spot, back to the highway. I'm walking up the dirt road, about fifty yards from the main road, wondering when I'm going to get jumped by some Miami hoodlums dumping a body—our outfitter has told us this is a favorite area for body dumping. (Of course, the same could be said for pretty much all of South Florida.) Anyway, I'm glancing around nervously when a patrol car careens onto my little road. I keep walking, though slower. Oddly, the cop car appears to speed up and it's headed right for me.

I decide it's best to stop and wave. It keeps coming—now just twenty feet away. I wave some more.

Both cops hop out of the car, guns pointing directly at me.

"What are you doing here, sir?" one screams.

"I . . . I'm putting in here."

"What?" They're just a few feet away now, still covering me with their guns.

"Uh, I'm going poling across the saw grass for a week or so."

They look at me in that cop sort of way, as if to say this answer isn't good enough. I take off my straw hat.

"I'm waiting for a park ranger who's going with us. Steve Robinson. He should be here any minute."

Inconceivably and just as suddenly, they say "OK," put their guns away, and drive off. Maybe they've noticed my Tevas. What kind of killer wears Tevas?

Steve shows up about fifteen minutes later, and within an hour or so we are on our way. Hugh Willoughby, author of *Across the Everglades,* who traversed the Everglades with a local fisherman, moonshiner, poaching plume hunter named David Brewer in 1898, gave the order for their journey to officially proceed—an odd bit of theatrics given it was just the two of them on the expedition. So I do the same.

"I give the order to proceed."

"It looks like we're setting off into a bush," David says. David didn't mean "the" bush; he meant what he said: a bush. David is a filmmaker and he's shooting with his digital video camera while launching his boat with Saranne. "I've never put in anywhere like this." It's a wall of willows and invasive Brazilian pepper plants. It's hard to imagine that the boats are going to float, not to mention squeeze through the brush. Yet, somehow, we're able to move.

We go two and a half miles that afternoon with me panicking the entire time. I've never poled before, and the heavy PVC pipes that Outward Bound has lent us are not making things too easy. I find myself glancing resentfully at Steve, who's in a light Kevlar canoe and pushing his boat along with an equally light pole of his own devising. Saranne and David are together, so they're moving along pretty easily, too. When the first higher batch of saw grass requires me to use all my weight and bend the pole nearly double just to keep moving, I nearly shout, "Wait! Wait, you damned idiots! We might get separated." The saw grass is so high I can't see which way they've turned. A minute later I'm glad I didn't. I've caught up with them and Steve is telling me, "You gotta go with the flow, here. Don't fight it. Less is more. That's what works in the Everglades."

I consider whacking him over the head with my pole but realize we're doomed without him, so instead, I whack myself. Actually, I don't so much whack myself as cause my body to exit my canoe while still maintaining a tight grip on my pole. My canoe shoots forward as I land on my back in the water and then my pole hits me.

While I don't keep this new perspective for long—this is my first day and I'm still deathly afraid of alligators and snakes—I stay half-submerged long enough to realize that I am surrounded by the softest scene, the softest light, the softest water I've ever encountered. This water, just a few miles from the Tamiami Trail, is not only clear but it's pH neutral. You know those fantasies you have where you duck beneath a gargantuan waterfall and all your troubles are washed away—like in that Irish Spring commercial (or was that in the Old Spice ad)? That water sucks. This is the stuff. Imagine what it was like back in the womb, surrounded and coddled by all that nurturing amniotic fluid. Well, I don't have to. I'm lying in that oasis right now, and I'm able to pause just long enough—about a second, on account of the alligators—to soak it all in.

And the sun is doing something really weird. It's creating the most mellow, golden aura. There is probably a scientific reason for it, having to do with refraction and reflection, but it seems as if the light advances through and over the pale green saw grass, plays along the surface of the periphyton-rich waters, and then dives down to the dark, mucky bottom, and from there spreads back up to the surface to engulf the Everglades and our little group. When I catch back up to my canoe and climb back in, I'm basked—not as in "basked in" but just simply basked. Jesus, Muhammed, and the Buddha together in a hot tub couldn't make me feel more comforted.

We raft our canoes together that night in a small pond. By pond, I mean a small area about half the size of a football field where the saw grass pokes just a foot above the surface, making for easy maneuvering. Rafting together takes about an hour, and consists of tying the boats together by stretching paddles and poles across the bow and stern and tying them down to the canoes and then laying plywood boards two-and-a-half feet wide and eight or so feet long across the top of the canoes. (The boards sit in the bottom of our canoes during the day.) Steve, although he opts for sleeping in his canoe alone, helps David, Saranne, and me make our bed, which will also serve as our kitchen and dining room.

Although the river's flow is nearly imperceptible—my spit takes more than a minute to travel from one end of the canoe to the other—it's apparently enough to discourage the mosquitoes. Not a single bite. We pump our water straight out of the river, but it travels through a carbon camp filter before it enters our bottles. I want to drink it straight. Once again, I find myself envious of Hugh Willoughby: "The popular impression has always been that the Everglades is a huge swamp, full of malaria and disease germs. There was certainly nothing in our surroundings that would remind one of a swamp. . . . I had no hesitation in drinking it whenever the canoe stopped, taking two or three glasses at a time, when thirsty from the exertion of poling. It agreed with Brewer and myself perfectly; we did not know a sick hour from this or any other cause."

The next day I become more adjusted to the poling. The

only time I really freak out is when the rest of us get separated from Steve. We've been following his lead, but after a while David and I start to think we can see things as well as he does. At the north end of a hammock—dry land created by thousands of years of decaying saw grass and other matter, now densely forested with palm trees, bay trees, poisonwood, melaleuca (sometimes), pond apples, among others—we go right, but Steve goes left. Saw grass is densest around hammocks. It actually becomes impenetrable to poling, and you have to get out and push your canoe. This we discover when we try to cut across the southern end of the hammock. A typical hammock is tear shaped—with the upstream section being the fat end of the tear as the result of current dynamics. Inexplicably I reason that the downstream side, besides being tapered, will also have less growth near its shores. I have reasoned incorrectly. It's worse. We spend more than ninety minutes trying to get back to Steve, who is only two hundred yards to our east. The panicked state created by this predicament—the uncontrollable thoughts of our getting lost, starving, and finally, dying—is worth noting only in that it was there.

The upside to getting separated is that while we're staring up at the sky cursing our fate, we see four snail kites—the endangered raptor that lives solely on the apple snail—and better yet, we watch one successfully snatch a snail from a saw grass blade and transfer it in the air from claws to beak. As I watch, I almost don't feel sorry for the bird because of its lack of "plasticity," as today's scientists call adaptability. The snail kite is bound to go the way of the dodo or even the ivory-billed woodpecker, who only ate grubs beneath the bark of decaying trees—never live ones—in the southern U.S. forests. Once so many trees were chopped down and thus not allowed to decay, the woodpecker's favorite food source was gone. Since they had no "plasticity," within a short time the ivorybills were gone, too. It's the same for the snail kite, I'm thinking in my agitated state (having grown somewhat snarly from screaming for Steve at the top of my lungs). They could adapt to eating other snails, one would think, but hell, no. They're holding out for their strict, declining diet.

It occurs to me as we fight through saw grass to reconnect with Steve that maybe instead of raising Tamiami Trail to increase water supply and thus increase the length of time the apple snails can survive, we ought to just be raising apple snails and dumping them in the park. This is Florida; everything can be managed! Think of the money we'd save.

Needless to say our group doesn't make it very far on the second day—perhaps six miles—but we do end up at a welcome campsite: dry land. It's not really land, as in a hammock or shell mound, but instead, the dock for the old phosphate/nitrate testing station built twenty years back to show the effects of these nutrients on Everglades water. Amazingly, the effects are still glaringly obvious. There is no saw grass behind the chutes where the nutrients were loaded and no life-sustaining periphyton; yards and yards downstream of the chutes, there are only these floating green algae mats.

While we're staring down at these test sites, David asks Steve why he cares so much about the Everglades.

"When I was a kid, my granddad took me to the spot where he grew up—in what is now a part of the Tampa metropolis. There were some houses already there, but nothing like today. He told me how everything used to be absolutely pristine—right there. About the fishing he'd done. Well, I want to see through my eyes what he saw as a young man. You have to think there's a possibility."

"What? So you want to go backward? That's not what humans are about," David points out.

"I do want to go backward," Steve says, then takes an unexpected twist. "Back to a time when people in Florida could be prosperous. Our future is no longer bright. Overpopulation. Not enough water. Pollution. I can't help yearning for those days when the earth was healthier. To have a bright financial future, we need to go back to a time or place when there was a lot of water, fish, and birds. That's what makes this place financially viable. Look around. Do you see any fish? Birds?"

There's nothing—not a chirp, not a splash.

"I've been wading in waters like this my whole life— these waters and the ones that are no longer there up in Orlando. I've never seen so few fish. These were historically very productive waters. This new plan, while a wonderful step, isn't going to change any of that. We've 'saved' the Everglades five times since I've been around, and I haven't seen an improvement yet. They want to fix it the same way they broke it—water manipulation, control of nature. They don't want to allow natural fluctuations. 'My heavens, we can't do that. The animals and fish might die.' Well, I hate to break it to them, but that's already happened. I say, let nature take its course. If you can accomplish more by doing nothing, then do nothing. Open everything up and let the water flow."

With his long hair and gray beard he seems like a biblical figure standing there in the setting sun. Instead of chanting, "Let my people go," he's pleading for the heathens to do something just as simple, just as elemental: "Let my water flow."

"RRRAHHH! RRRAHHH!"

This is what we wake up to the next morning. It sounds

like the biggest frog I've ever heard—a cross between a lion and a human burp, or closer yet, a growling stomach magnified a thousand times.

"That's an alligator," Steve says, leaning onto one elbow. "It's a big daddy warning someone where his territory is. If you were a young male alligator, you'd listen to these sounds and then try to find a nice quiet spot far, far away. Eating small alligators is not so much a delicacy for larger alligators as a territorial necessity."

David is already up, putting on the headphones that are connected to his camera. It's a hot morning and he's sweating, rubbing his wrists, which are getting sore from the poling. "How about humans?" he asks when a closer, louder bellow emerges. He looks around in mock fear, but how much is he really playing? It's an intimidating sound.

"Evidently, we're not very tasty," Steve says. "An alligator would much sooner scurry away from a human than bite one. We present a pretty big profile, except when we're just dangling a limb in the water." I yank my left foot out of the river.

We eat breakfast to the sound of the growls, then start poling south/southeast to the growls. I fall face first in the water with a pole misplant to the accompaniment of the growls, scaring a two-foot alligator resting on a lily pad. It's almost like the old days when soldiers would enter the Everglades and smoke signals rose from one hammock to the other to warn of their approach. Our progress is radioed from one alligator to another all morning long.

"We're hearing the high part of the note of their growl," Steve explains. It's a very deep sound. Impossible to imagine anything much deeper or lower. "The bellow begins earlier with a much lower note that actually vibrates the water."

"Is that meant to be intimidating?" I ask.

"It's only informational, but if it sounds intimidating, then that's its info."

That is definitely the information I'm getting this morning. We pole on and on, and to my surprise the movement becomes rhythmic. I've adopted a much smoother plant and push and can keep up with Steve fairly easily now. It also helps that I've sneaked forty pounds of water into David and Saranne's canoe.

Trying for every possible experience in the Everglades, we decide to tackle a hammock called Panther Mound a little after lunch. From afar, it doesn't seem like a big deal, although we do have to go about a quarter-mile past it, then cut back northwest to get to its perimeter. Then a hundred yards out, or probably less, we abandon our canoes and start walking through a jungle, except this jungle is knee deep in water.

"It's completely unreal," Saranne says. She says this while holding back the branch of a poisonwood tree, which is, not surprisingly, poisonous to the touch. Since she's wearing gloves and is thus protected, I don't bother warning her. Also, this one looks a little like a gumbo-limbo tree or "tourist" tree—so called because its reddish bark peels like the skin of a sunbaked Yankee. I wouldn't want to warn her for nothing.

"Primordial," Steve adds, stalled in his tracks by a tangle of mangrove roots.

"Elemental," chimes in David.

"Disgusting," I say as my foot sinks about two feet into the bottomless muck.

Saranne leads with a running monologue of "Yes, this is quite difficult" and "We're almost there" and "I think I see land." What she finds difficult, we mortals find impossible, and after a while it becomes quite clear that she's not seeing dry land but some sort of morass-infused optical illusion. Steve begins to linger farther and farther behind even when we reach a two-board-wide boardwalk that heads toward the island. We rejoice momentarily over finding the board-walk (perhaps built by scientists many years back), until David falls through the first rotten board. Even so, we stick to the planks because the growth, while not stymied by any means, is sparser there.

After a knee-high wade at the boardwalk's end, followed by a short belly-button-deep trudge, we reach dry land. I've never been on a hammock before and it's not quite what I expect. I think I'd imagined an open meadow, surrounded by all the bushes and trees we've passed, perhaps shaded by a few towering royal palm trees and even a couple of pines. Instead, what we get is merely more jungle. The trees are low-slung and we have to crouch most of the time. Vines that might appeal to Tarzan drape the sky and hang to the ground.

"Limes," Saranne says. "They're all over the place."

"Key limes," I add, picking up the small fruit and biting into it, sucking it dry. "I love hunting and gathering."

"Um, I think it's foraging," David corrects and then turns his camera toward me, asking, "What are you doing, Hodding?" for his future audience.

"I know. I was joking, you dickwhack." Liking the attention, I guess, I launch into a bubbling description of the joys of foraging and gather up a few more limes and bite away. David then turns to Steve, who is carefully cutting away the top of a lime he's found.

"This is how my granddad did it," Steve says. "It's a natural juice box." Soon he's cleared a clean area for his lips and he sucks away joyfully.

"What kind of bone is this?" David asks moments later, holding up a deer jaw.

There are hundreds of bones—all in the central area under a sour orange tree. Something around here clearly likes deer and wild pig. Next we discover a sleeping nest; a bed, we realize, big enough for a bear or perhaps even a panther.

Then, and this is the most important discovery, we see the scat. How we've missed it up till now, I'll never know. But the large Ho Ho–size poops are everywhere. More important, they're scattered amongst the limes I've been gathering off the ground. Of course, I don't pay any attention to this connection at the time—not until a few days later when I'm having to use the bathroom every few minutes over the side of my canoe will I even begin to think about it, in fact.

"This is great!" I say. "There's scat everywhere."

"What's so great about that?" David asks, camera on. It's not until those few days later that I realize just why he's smiling. At the time I assume he's as excited as me because we can figure out what kind of animal lives there.

"Well, these scats can only be from a large carnivorous or omnivorous animal," I say. "There's hairs and some sort of fibrous materials in here." And I peel apart a scat. "This part of the Everglades can still sustain some large animal that is dining on what the place has to offer. Isn't that great!"

"Yes, it is, Hodding," Steve says. "But we should be seeing signs like this on every mound, but my bet is we wouldn't." We can't find any scratch marks around the scat, like a cat typically makes, but we also don't find any bear prints.

Steve points to a scat that can't be more than a day or so old, judging by the bugs and moistness.

CRACK!

"What's that?" David asks and whips his camera

around. His footage later reveals Steve and me simultaneously jerking our heads around as well.

Suddenly we decide it's best to leave the hammock. For
the animal's sake, of course—not because we're scared or
anything, but because we know how few places any
Everglades animal has to live. The Florida panther is so
endangered that for most purposes, they're extinct. Less
than eighty panthers live in the wild, and a lot of these are
the offspring of cougars brought in from Texas. They're not
purebred Florida panthers, although panthers, cougars,
pumas, and mountain lions are virtually the same species:
Felis concolor, cat of one color. It's so bad that the media
recently made a big deal about the first panther seen in
Hillsborough County (between Tampa and Saint
Petersburg) in nearly thirty years, and they were talking
about roadkill, found dead along Interstate 4. And while
black bears aren't endangered in Florida, there aren't very
many in the Everglades. Steve's never seen one in the park,
for instance.

The next few days are more of the same, as far as the saw
grass goes, except that I find out why the saw grass hasn't
become "Swimming Hole No. 1" on everybody's "Must
Swim" list. It's the morning of Day 4 of our trip. We're pushing through a particularly difficult stretch of saw grass—so
difficult that everybody, including Steve, is in the water
shoving his/her canoe forward. I'm grumbling to myself,
thinking about all the wrongs inflicted upon me, when
David suddenly starts screaming, "Ow! Ow! OW!" And
frantically dives into his canoe, yanks off his shoe and starts
rubbing his foot as if it's the end of the world. I, of course,
immediately brighten.

"What's wrong, you big baby? Got a cramp?" I ask, as
unsympathetically as possible. I chuckle even.

"No, something bit my foot. It's killing me," he answers seriously, as if it's a matter of life or death. I glance at the offended limb but see nothing but a tiny blemish. I chuckle some more. I also take this moment as a chance to line my boat directly behind his and Saranne's so they have to break the trail first.

A few minutes later David hops back in and we trudge on. The pain is gone. I'm still chuckling when I'm zapped with a bolt of searing electricity on top of my right foot, inside my shoe.

"Yaowww!" I scream. I dive into my aluminum canoe, scraping my shin hard enough to draw blood, and yank off my shoe even faster than David had. I've been bitten, too. It feels like ten bees have stung me at once and the bite sends shivers across my body. I'm thinking I've got to get out of here; that no way can I keep going with this kind of pain, and I rub the bite harder and harder. Woe is me. Within a few minutes, though, the pain's vanished. I ease back into the water, momentarily humbled.

I ask Steve and Saranne if they've been bitten. "Not today," Steve says. "But I have in the past. I don't know what kind of bug it is, but it hurts." Later, a scientist will tell me it's called an alligator bug and that he never goes wading in saw grass because of its sting.

"Yes," Saranne answers, "I was bitten a few moments ago. It did hurt a while." Realizing that she had said nothing at the time, I'm humbled a bit longer.

The going gets easier later that day because we run into the airboat trail that all the scientists use. It's hard to say how many scientists work in the park, but they're from all over: park employees, SFWMD people, Fish and Wildlife, Florida universities, other universities, and foreign schools and organizations. We run into two such scientists from

Florida International University one afternoon: Shawna Baker, who is getting her master's in wetland ecology, and Travis Tuten, a field technician, planning on getting his master's as well.

"I love it out here," Travis offers. He is stroking the saw grass as he speaks. "How peaceful it is. Makes me happy." Travis is from Orlando. "I never came to the Everglades until I got this job. I used to think of it as a whole bunch of swampy trees—cypresses and stuff. It's so different than the way I thought it'd be. I didn't think it'd be so clean."

Still that same day, we reach an exceptional spot called Rookery Branch where Shark River Slough pretty much becomes Shark River and branches to the southwest. The water turns into what we commonly understand as a river. It has a channel. It's relatively deep—five feet or so—and like everywhere else in the Everglades, it's clear to the bottom. The bottom, though, is covered with broken shells. In addition to the saw grass, it's bordered by pond-apple trees, arrowheads, pickerelweed with its iridescent purple flowers, and pond lilies with their bright offerings of yellow blossoms.

Huge bass shake the river's surface. A little blue heron, still in its white phase, swoops down for a landing and then, spying us, flaps out of there as fast as it can. The wind rushing through the saw grass sounds like the constant shake of a baby's rattle.

We ease out of our canoes and swim up and down a long expanse of the river, fighting against the current and then riding it back on our backs. The feeling is luxurious and special. I wish that Stu Appelbaum, Senator Graham, the park public relations people who give me standard issue answers, Dave Swift from SFWMD, the sugar farmer Russell Kilpatrick, and even Jeb Bush could be floating on their backs with me. Maybe it would show or remind them what the place is.

The going gets tough again after our swim. There's an airboat trail marked on our maps, and every once in a while we see a real life marker, but it seems that most people don't come this way, "this way" being where we've left the main flow of Shark River Slough and branched off to the south/southeast to make our attempt at reaching Florida Bay. Shark River eventually dumps into the Gulf of Mexico, but the saw-grass prairie we're cutting across traditionally brought fresh water to Florida Bay. In my imagination it is this water that once made the bay so healthy and bountiful, such a great breeding ground for fish, birds, and sharks.

Sweating from trying to keep my boat moving forward after each pass with the pole instead of coming to a standstill, I start swimming every chance I get, having lost all fear of the saw grass and its unseen dangers despite the alligator bugs. The going is so tough—we make about two hundred yards an hour—that I have to do something to sustain hope.

The wind is blowing hard from the north—probably fifteen to twenty knots.

"Maybe we should sail," David jokes. I've talked to some park service people who have sailed in specially rigged canoes and kayaks down the airboat trail we are on then out onto Shark River and then into the Gulf. All we have is a large plastic tarp, but we give it a try—at first somewhat halfheartedly. Then as we actually begin to move, and then move even faster than when we were poling, we get more serious, more elaborate, and cruise down the saw grass, managing the sail by rigging it as a sideways square sail: Our poles are attached to the outer edges, which we hold on to while leaning backward. It doesn't last very long and it's definitely no Viking ship, but it's fun, and soon

213

we're at the mangrove fringe that hides the entrance to North River. We've gone about twenty-five miles since setting off from the Tamiami Trail and have at least that many more to cover before we reach the bay.

It's Day 5 and our plan is to find our way through the freshwater mangroves to the North River, follow it through a series of other rivers and streams that will take us down to the park road, where a minimally maintained canoe trail begins on the other side that we can follow to the bay. Simple enough, except for the mangroves, of course.

We spend the day poling the perimeter, trying to twist into the deeper pockets of water that form where the mangroves meet the saw grass, while we look for our stream. Eventually, I think I've found it and lead David and Saranne into the darkness. Steve has stayed behind, suggesting we might be wasting our time. After twenty minutes of poling and increasingly encroaching mangrove limbs and roots we reach our first dead end. We've only gone a few hundred yards, but I think I can see clear water ahead. Excited by a chance to use a tool, to bash my way through the jungle, I grab David's saw and begin cutting. The mangrove limb is only five inches thick but sawing through it takes much longer than I'd hoped. Ten or so minutes later, my arm burning, we scrape our canoes through the new opening.

"I've got to hand it to you, Hodding. You were right," David says as we pole and paddle through the now widening stream. I'm all happy and start singing "A-marching we will go." Saranne, who's usually so bubbly, keeps quiet. A few minutes later we run into a tangled mess of mangrove roots, limbs, and crisscrossing spiderwebs that looks at least ten feet thick.

"I think we'd better turn back, boys," Saranne says. "It

might be clear on the other side, but we should get back, set up camp. Looks like Steve might be right." Having climbed a mangrove branch for a better view, I point out it's clear beyond this second patch, but we agree to turn around. This is just a scouting mission for the next day's hard push, and we've probably already gone a half mile. We only have to cover six miles the next day. It shouldn't be too hard—a little sawing, some pulling the canoes over forgiving roots, perhaps an alligator scare or two. Considering we've just done half a mile in such a short amount of time, I think it should be easy enough.

That night I lie on my plywood board unable to sleep, and as I squirm in my sleeping sack, continually pushing the mosquito netting away from my face so they'll stop biting my face, I'm reminded of Willoughby's sleeplessness: "Everything had been so desolate and quiet during the day that that one would naturally think the stillness of the night would be quite appalling. But as the hours advanced new combinations of sounds broke upon the ear . . . the worst sound to sleep through is the cry of the limpkin. When do these birds sleep? We have seen them almost all day and they seemed like a quiet, well-behaved bird, but their conduct at night is something most disreputable. I would drop off into a doze, conquering the other sounds, but as soon as a limpkin would screech I would be wide awake at once."

Our nights are silent, except for the mosquitoes and the infrequent bark of a pig frog. The limpkins, like so many other birds that used to nest and feed here, are gone. Come to think of it, even our days are silent, except for the bellowing alligators. However, historically, this part of the Everglades—the middle of the saw grass—never teemed with wildlife in the way that we imagine such things. That's why the Calusa never lived within the saw grass. So the silence is what it has always been. Except on the fringes, this place is and always has been a place of respite from the noise of the world.

Tonight, the mosquitoes are vicious, like they've never been, and they're much smaller—the dreaded salt marsh variety. Dreaded, because as the name implies, they breed in saltwater and don't need stagnant freshwater pools to multiply. Therefore, since we're closer to the coast now, there are millions; we can see tornadoes of them hovering over our heads. Although each bite reminds me how close we are to Florida Bay, I could happily remain a little less informed.

As the mosquitoes attack, Steve launches into an explanation of why there are more mosquitoes here, besides the fact that they're salt marsh mosquitoes. "Dragonflies need eight months to mature, and there are only six good months of water here due to the current water management practices. Mosquitoes are a dragonfly's favorite food." Not enough water means not enough dragonflies means way too many mosquitoes.

I can't sleep. The mosquitoes are certainly loud, but it also has something to do with David. Once again, he is swinging his arms because of his aching wrists. Apparently, he's done some kind of nerve damage to them. He's also taken up talking to himself. At some point he stops swinging and I look up, perhaps on account of the sudden calm. Our platform is still, allowing a defining moment to take shape. I see David, by the light of the moon, talking to, I believe, his hands. At first I can't hear him, but after a while his words come across. In a pained, troubled mumble, he is repeating again and again, "The Hands, the Hands . . . oh, the Hands."

Our own Kurtz.

The next morning, Day 6, frantic squawks accompanied by guttural grunts and squeals wake us. A bird is under attack in the saw grass. We hear the shrieks, the chase, and finally nothing. So much stays hidden in the Everglades.

Saranne's the morning's cook—she and I are doing all the cooking, David and Steve, the washing—and she slips David more pancakes than the rest of us, which I smart about until I realize she's doing it for her own good. She's poling and paddling their canoe whenever he's filming or preparing his camera, so she needs to make sure he has enough stamina to help out the rest of the time. Either that, or she merely likes David more than Steve and me. Retaliating, I slip some of my research books, stored in a dry bag, under David's seat, along with one of the five-gallon water containers.

We enter the mangroves again. Being hardened veterans of the Everglades, we travel fast, covering the first quarter mile in thirty minutes; we'll be out of the mangroves by sunset. Giddy, I make the mistake of telling Saranne about sneaking extra weight into their boat and have to take the water back. Soon enough, we're pushing, dragging, bending our canoes through an endless series of S-turns, where the distance of the run is only as long as the canoe, making for bone-wrenching curse-filled maneuvering. Again and again, we must step into the brown water and literally wrestle the canoes around less and less forgiving mangroves.

The water is brownish-black from tannin and rot. In places it comes up to our chests and the methane bubbles burst up from the river's floor with each step we take, surrounding us with nature's farts. I briefly consider the probable fact that we might be the only humans who ever walked in this spot. We're certainly the first white ones to do so, and I really hope we'll live to tell about it. When the mangroves let us through, orbed weavers ensnare us in their sticky webs. The spiders look beautifully danger-

217

ous—the way most super-poisonous things do, like coral snakes—but like their less colorful cousins, these arachnids prefer bugs to humans. There would be no relief to the horrors of this part of the journey if it weren't for the little green tree frogs, falling from the rubbery branches, that ride on our shoulders. We keep telling each other that all we have to do is cover six miles, then we'll be on those more frequented navigable rivers, the last of which, Alligator Creek, flows into Florida Bay. Desperately, I want to see freshwater meeting salt, to reach the terminus of all these troubled waters.

By noon we've slowed considerably, covering roughly a hundred yards in an hour, according to the GPS. The river has widened and we've even passed two confluences, but now mangrove roots have plopped down everywhere. We can't go more than ten yards without using the saw. At two-thirty, despite not resting for more than thirty minutes for lunch, we've gone less than a mile for the day. The last fifty yards has taken us forty-five minutes to cover. Now, a jungly forest of mangroves covers the entire width of the stream, and it looks at least twenty yards deep. We can't see through them to open water—something we've always been able to do up to this point.

I climb a withered mangrove trunk to spy a possible route forward. I can see a pool not too far ahead that we couldn't see from water level. Then I look farther down and it's worse, much much worse. On a whim I look back the way we've been trudging all day. To my utter astonishment, I can see a discernible watercourse for a long, long ways back, and I know it gets even easier after that. I look downstream again. I see nothing but mangroves.

We give up and decide to turn around. Steve has to be back to work in two days. David is supposed to fly home in three. It's hopeless, making it this way. The mangroves have beaten me again, just like they did when my friend Russell and I tried to paddle down the park's Everglades Waterway without any food.

It takes about half as long getting back out of our dead-end stream as it took getting in. Going back isn't as physically hard, but it's pretty rough mentally. No one talks much. It crosses my mind how fast we've adapted to our surroundings, though. I'm not glancing around for the next cottonmouth or the clamping jaws of an irate alligator while I trudge in chest-high pools. I'm not even worried about snakes dropping out of the trees.

"Any snakes dropping out of trees in the Everglades won't be poisonous. You might have to brush them off of you, but otherwise, don't worry," Steve had said earlier in the day. I think back to Willoughby, going on about trying to find some mythical giant snake that was supposed to live in the Everglades. There was no such species and on top of that, pretty much all the snakes he killed were the drop-from-the-tree variety and therefore, harmless.

Out in the open many hours later, tied up to the same fledgling mangroves we camped next to the night before, we decide we can't attempt the mangrove route again, for the same reasons that stopped us earlier in the day—people have their "real" lives to consider.

"My only concern is that Hodding might consider this mutiny," Saranne says. "Do you?"

Yes, I answer, but add that it's welcome in some ways because it means we get to return to the saw grass; I'll take saw grass over mangroves any day. I appear to be making a habit of getting my butt kicked by the Everglades and am comforted by the thought that there's some meaning in this repetition of failure, only I'm too tired to figure it out. I have my best sleep of the trip that night.

We spend two more days poling in what becomes increasingly shallow water. Nonetheless, I float on my back in any open patch that presents itself, unable to get enough of this perfect water, knowing that I might never again have the chance to luxuriate in what has become my favorite water in the world.

The Everglades might be shallow down here, but it's so clean because it relies on its own rainwater. Thanks to the canals and levees that separate the lower Everglades from its traditional water supply from what is now the Everglades Agricultural Area, most of the polluted runoff from the sugarcane farms, cattle ranches, and citrus orchards bypasses anything below the Tamiami Trail, which means that in an ironic twist of fate, the Everglades National Park is the healthiest part of the ecosystem precisely because it *doesn't* receive its historical flow. The water conservation areas above the Tamiami Trail and all of Florida Bay may be sick, but as long as South Florida receives its average sixty inches of rainfall, the park part of the Everglades is getting by, more or less. I share my thoughts with the others.

"Some scientists believe the lower Everglades always had a dry period," Steve says on the last day as we pole past impressive cypress stands along the final few miles before we reach the park road. "But a dryout only allows for small fish. We know that once there were big fish here. I think water is here year-round except in the driest of years. In that scenario, you had high water nesting, and the birds that have now disappeared had a reason to stay here."

So, no one agrees on anything in the Everglades. That's not a big surprise by this point. And it doesn't really matter because the old Everglades is clearly gone forever. The new

Everglades, though, is on its way, with its high-tech new wells, massive pumps, and readjusted canals.

Later that afternoon of Day 8, we intersect the park road, unceremoniously hitch a ride to Flamingo, and the trip is over. Steve puts us up in his apartment in Flamingo—one of many cinderblock apartments built one story above the ground that the park provides for its employees.

After a good night's sleep, discounting the hour I lay awake watching David swing his arms (yes, even on dry land he was still doing it; pity his poor wife), Saranne, Steve, and I decide to take the canoes out into the bay the next day and head toward Alligator Creek's mouth, hugging the southern mangrove shore. We'd hoped to exit the Everglades via Alligator Creek, so it seems fitting to conclude our trip there anyway.

We're casually paddling past acres of guano-covered mangroves, overwhelmed with the stench of so much avian waste product, when rain begins pounding the bay a quarter mile away where we can see a shark hunting in the shallows. The rain sounds like a magnificent waterfall, and the moment becomes one of those memories that's etched into your brain forever.

As if on command, roseate spoonbills soar straight above us. When they're directly overhead, their color darkens to a deep, rich pink. Mangrove islands shimmer in the heat way to the southeast. A reddish egret darts madly about for some fleeing prey in the shallows, looking deranged. It hops, runs, twists sideways, dives, and trips over its own legs chasing its lunch, and we burst out laughing—the thing literally looks insane to us.

Pelicans stare down from the mangroves just to our left. Then two hundred plovers come swooping down God-

221

knows-how-fast, shrieking just a few feet over our heads, making us swing around with fright. Two birds, not too sure which way to go around my head, miss me by inches.

"They all charge out at once for protection," Steve explains. "It's harder for preying birds to pick one out."

Mullet are jumping high in the air or charging at something just beneath the surface—but they're always beside us. We can't see them underwater, though, on account of the bay being so muddy. Where it's not muddy, it's cloudy.

"Eighty percent of this bay used to be covered with turtle grass. The grass would use the diatoms as nutrients," Steve says. "Now, the diatoms just die, unused because pollution and boats have destroyed the turtle grass. They sink to the bottom and create the ever-thickening mud. The bay used to accumulate about an inch of this mud every hundred years. We've gotten two feet in the last twenty years. We should be seeing turtle grass everywhere."

Hell, I can't see more than an inch below the surface. This is worse than I imagined. Maybe Steve's right, after all, about the destructive nature of a shallower lower Everglades. If the freshwater were still seeping through the mangroves directly into the bay, as it did in the past, and not either held back interminably or released in a massive flood because of some court-ordered schedule, then, according to most scientists, the bay would be clear again.

If the Comprehensive Plan isn't going to fix this, then what, or who, can?

The Politician

I T'S SIMPLE REALLY. IT'S ALL IN HOW WE VOTE. IT'S WHOM we choose to make the decisions for us. The answer is there: Just look at who you've picked for mayor, legislator, senator, and president. We get what we deserve.

Just like fifty years ago, when America first asked the Corps to solve the Everglades drainage problem, the Corps' current response is a reflection of our will, our sensibilities. One hundred years earlier than that, Buckingham Smith reflected his times by going against his nonpragmatic side and voicing a judgment that the Everglades should and could be drained.

And now it seems we're all about image. It doesn't matter what actually happens, as long as you toe the line. The public is out front, clicking its emerald heels together, wishing, wishing, wishing but not bothering to follow up.

Senator Bob Graham is the point man for the Everglades in the U.S. Senate. He's been a Florida lawyer, a state legislator, a governor, and a U.S. senator. If it were the Florida voters' will, and ours, he could straighten things out, whether he truly cares about it or not.

And if Graham really cared all on his own about the fate of the Everglades, he could still fight for the Comprehensive Plan to be whatever he wants it to be. The Everglades really could still be redirected to resemble its historic self, something closer to what Steve Robinson hopes for.

On a quiet Sunday morning in February, I arrive by taxi in Graham Country, a development called Miami Lakes that has taken over what used to be part of the Everglades. We're going to ride together to the Delray Beach Marriott, where Graham will give the keynote speech at the annual Everglades Coalition meeting.

Miami Lakes feels like a movie set, resembling something European with its balconies and railings. The streets are empty, and even though it's sunny as usual, it's a little spooky. It makes me feel lost.

The Grahams have owned this land since early in the twentieth century, when Senator Graham's father came down to run the Pennsuco Sugar Company's operations. The company eventually went out of business and the senior Graham bought the land at a discount and started a lucrative cattle operation.

I wait for Graham outside the Don Shula Hotel. There's a goalpost out front, taken from the Dolphins training field, the year I was a Dolphins fan—1972. (They were cool back then—they had Mercury Morris.)

Graham arrives right on time, dressed in a light gray flannel suit, white shirt, dark blue tie with some kind of white birds on it, done up a little short. He's driving a weathered blue 1994 Chrysler Concorde.

"You're the young man, Hodding Carter?" he says after we gesture to each other as he pulls up in the car. "You'll have to excuse me a moment. I need to make a trip to the men's room," he says as I open the passenger door. I look around. The leather seats are worn, the floors coffee-stained with scattered gravel. Forty-eight thousand miles on the odometer. The car fits my image of Graham and I'm pleased. At least he's not one of those types who want to look hip but miss horribly. His head looks like Graham, but his body seems smaller than I recall, something TV does to people, I guess. We don't shake hands—he's focused on getting to the bathroom—doesn't talk to anyone on the way in, his head down.

Coming out, he's heads up and he's immediately recognized—first by a lobbyist who hails him. Graham yells back, "What are you doing with such an expensive car?" and walks over to him. One slings an arm over the other's shoulder. They're talking about what golf courses are best, and a new one they haven't tried. I can't make out much of what they're saying, except that the lobbyist wants him to run for president. Graham tells him he doesn't believe Hussein has nuclear arms. At the end of their confab, the lobbyist mentions his son is looking for a job; currently interning for someone else, but he'd really like for his son to work for Graham. "It's the direction I hope he'll go." Graham doesn't commit, performs the "hand-on-the-other-guy's-arm" parting, and is hailed again before he reaches the car by a black woman with a foreign accent.

Graham says hello, then immediately asks her where she's from, originally. She answers Haiti and he turns consoling, expressing sorrow over the condition of some particular Haitian children. I'm not sure what children he's talking about, but he's got her. Actually, he already had her, but this makes things warmer. They depart. Then she comes running back before he can shut his door completely, asking if he's taking contributions for his presidential campaign yet. He isn't officially running, but later that day he'll tell some reporters, "I'm going to be the next president of the United States."

The first fifteen minutes of our conversation revolve around Miami Lakes. We're driving down Main Street—curving neo-Florida, Old World–wannabe architecture, with wrought iron here and there, those balconies mentioned earlier, and everything plastered with stucco. Lots of stucco.

It's *almost* charming, and Graham seems tickled by it. He talks about his family owning the land for seventy years and how in the mid-fifties, suburbs grew to the edge of their farm. His voice and demeanor are light, carefree.

"Dad wanted to sell," Graham explains, "but my first and second oldest brothers and I thought we could do something ourselves, so we asked him if we could try something different. We started researching and were drawn to the 'New Town' concept. Back then there were two schools of New Town thought: British and Scandinavian. The British involved moving huge sums of people out of the cities and depositing them somewhere. The Scandinavian idea was to give order to a metro area. We liked the Scandinavian model better and this street—have you ever been to Copenhagen? Seen the Walking Street? [I nod.] Well, this is almost the exact dimensions of that street. We stole all of our good ideas from them."

He knows his facts and figures and they come reeling out: 23,000 residents, five churches, every twenty to thirty homesites have a small park. Fifteen thousand people come work here and of the 23,000 residents, 15 percent work in Miami Lakes, most of the rest in the city. The whole development covers about five sections—three thousand acres.

"We've just about finished the last of the residential stage. No more houses will go up after that, and then we'll move into the second phase of the Town Center." He expresses real disappointment that the New Town movement didn't catch on in the United States. His enthusiasm is infectious, although a bit incongruous. We're supposed to be talking about a subject that could be perceived as antithetical to development, I remind myself: environmental restoration.

To warm things up a bit, I tell him a story that Brandy Ayers, an Alabama newspaperman and family friend, has just told me the night before. After meeting Graham on an organizing trip for a fence-mending group back in the seventies, Brandy ran into Bob Graham's sister-in-law, Kay Graham, the publisher of *Newsweek* and *The Washington Post* at the time. Perhaps looking for something to speak with Kay Graham about and being a natural provocateur, Brandy said to her: "He is one of the brightest, nicest young politicians I've come across." She looked at Brandy without saying a word, wondering why this man was buttering her up. Then, after a long-enough pause, Brandy added, "Yep, the brightest fellow and the most unelectable politician I've ever come across."

Brandy then explained to me what saved Graham as far as the unelectable thing went were Graham's Workdays, a seemingly heartfelt device he still uses today to stay in touch with real Floridians. He works for an entire day at an ordinary job, learning and talking about the issues of his fellow workers.

I tell this story to Graham, who laughs. But I omit the bit

about the Workdays. However, without missing a beat, he begins to tell the story of how he started his Workdays program. He knows the date, the school, and the teacher's name who pushed him into the idea—a woman who said to him, after he'd given a talk as the minority chair of the state education committee, "I am sick to death of you politicians talking about things you don't know anything about." In his response, he asked her how he was supposed to find out. He gave it no more thought, but ten days later the teacher contacted him; she'd made arrangements for him to teach in Room 200 at the Carroll City High School: "You'll be teaching twelfth grade Civics for the next eighteen weeks."

He took the challenge, set up a syllabus with a young black teacher, and had an "incredible" experience.

"I got a real grounded sense in learning about the life of a teacher. And I realized if it worked in that field it'd probably work in others and that's how I started my Workdays. So I'm aware of what Brandy is alluding to. These Workdays had an altering effect on me in that I became prepared, connected. I could speak from having learned from reality." His 387th job is next Friday at Patrick Air Force Base. The one after that will be building a kiosk at Loxahatchee. It will be the first kiosk of the new "Everglades Trail." This is a driving trail that he's been pushing recently to draw people into the Everglades area.

"One of the most difficult jobs I've done is working along the Tamiami Trail. I was working on one of the culverts that allow water into the Everglades, with some Seminole Indians. What they were really good at was doing the underwater work. It was amazing how those men could dive down and take these sandbags out."

Mod waters, the act passed to bring healthier amounts of water to the southeastern Everglades, was supposed to affect the area where Graham worked on the culverts so I ask him for his reaction to its holdup.

"It has been so frustrating," he says, twisting toward me, although keeping his eyes on the road. "It's an area that was never supposed to be developed. The Corps doesn't have eminent domain, so we're trying to get it for them. The new chairman of the EW has gotten the appropriations committee to remove it from the Department of the Interior's budget. Right now all of the resistance comes from the chairman."

At first Graham won't even mention the new chairman's name—Senator Inhofe, the Republican from Oklahoma who was also the only person in Congress to vote against the Comprehensive Plan. "This chairman is part of this western private-property-rights belief that any additional purchase of land by the federal government is automatically a bad idea and particularly if it's a nonconsensual taking."

(A month later the courts will clear the way for the Interior Department to take the land under eminent domain. Dexter Lehtinen, the former U.S. attorney who filed the 1988 lawsuit against the SFWMD that began this restoration process and who's been involved in Everglades restoration in one way or another since the beginning of the movement, then challenges the court ruling, and up until the fall of 2003, the 8-$\frac{1}{2}$ Square Milers are still there.)

I steer us back to the restoration plan and point out that people believe the plan will return natural flow to the Everglades and that they're going to be disappointed because that isn't going to happen.

"I believe I was the first person to articulate the phrase *Save our Everglades* back in 1983. Our standard was that the Everglades should look more like it did around 1900 than it did in 1983. I recognized that we're never going to make the

Everglades look like it did before development." He goes into the history of the Everglades and flood control. Then he says something that rings painfully true. "They should publish your book in a three-ring binder because it's going to be such a changing story. It always has been. The Everglades is a function of our values." He describes the changing values from Disston on down through to the Corps to the current idea of what he labels "trusteeship," explaining it wasn't until the 1970s, maybe the sixties, that the attitude started to shift toward trusteeship.

I ask him if he thinks this value system will up and change again. What I am wondering, but don't add at the time, is: Is this a part of our evolution as a species? Are we becoming more responsible—given that the majority of people wants this place to be restored? Or are we just fooling ourselves—just like Wescott, Smith, Bloxham, Broward, and all the rest?

"It's important to broaden the knowledge and experience of the American people in the Everglades so there will be a base of support in the same way there is a base of support in cleaning up the air over the Grand Canyon. We used to refer to it as Florida's Everglades, now we refer to it as America's Everglades, to emphasize this is a national treasure. Remember, this is a three-ringed binder. The other thing is the actual engineering of the American Everglades restoration. One of the reasons my colleague gave for not supporting restoration is that unlike most Corps projects, the Corps couldn't come in with dozens of maps and machines to show exactly how it'll look. He thinks there is too much uncertainty. In fact there is a lot of uncertainty, and that's because we're still discovering new things. So many of the projects are about testing out ideas. If they work, they'll go into full utilization. If they don't work, they'll try to figure out another way to do it. That disturbs some people, but I think it's the rational way to go about it."

We've gotten off of Interstate 95 and are driving by a strip mall that sits on what used to be the eastern edge of the Everglades. I remind him that environmentalists have the same concerns—that there aren't enough concrete projects and that no committee that knows anything has the power to reject or approve the projects.

"I know that concern. But I think it's Congress's responsibility, as overseers of this project."

I tell him about my talks with the two Stuarts and Alan Farago.

"We haven't had what I call a gray director of the Jacksonville Corps in fifteen years. Jacksonville is fortunate to get the first of this new wave starting with Rock Salt. He deserves a lot of credit for moving this thing forward." Rock Salt (yes, that's his name) was the director of the Corps during the nineties' restudy; many blame him for interpreting Congress's authorization to develop a plan for restoration as, instead, an authorization to find the best solution for agriculture and development while merely improving the Everglades' ecology.

I tell Graham that he seems to want to help the Everglades, but he's also clearly a developer. Alan Farago has asked me to ask Graham if he's willing to return Miami Lakes to the Everglades as an example of what others who've developed on the traditional Everglades should do. I don't go this far, but I do remind him that he's supported by agriculture.

"One of the candidates running for president was asked and apparently he couldn't answer, what philosopher has been most influential to him. My answer is John Stuart Mill. [Mill's principle of utility was: "Actions are right in proportion as they tend to promote happiness; wrong as they tend to produce the reverse of happiness."] Because I'm very much a pragmatist. I don't see the world as a series of yellow or green and red lights. It's much more complicated than that. A lot of people at this conference think the sugar industry is the devil, and it's true they've done some bad and insensitive things, no question about it, but what would have been better than sugar as a use for this land? In fact, it is one of the least polluting activities, and to the degree that it does pollute, and it does, it is one of the most correctable. It could've been dairy cows. We have a dairy farm west of the Everglades. Dairy cows have the unfortunate biological necessity to urinate and defecate. Imagine that stuff going into the Everglades."

He breaks off to ask me directions. I've got his schedule in hand, which includes step-by-step driving directions. It also tells him what to wear—in this case a business suit. (Later, Nat Reed, Nixon's Undersecretary of the Interior and a former board member of the SFWMD, will lament the good old days when a suit would have been the last thing one might see at one of these coalition meetings.)

We're nearing Linton Boulevard, and he suddenly seems more energetic. "We had four of them living right there. The hijackers. Right there and we didn't know it." Later, I read that this is a favorite subject of his—that he tends to see hijackers around every corner, or something like that. So it's probably no coincidence his next Workday is going to be at the high-security Patrick Air Force Base where they work on decoding intercepted messages.

"Setting aside pragmatism, is there anything special about the Everglades that appeals to you, that gives you a connection to it?"

"If you went four miles due west, you'd come to the little town of Pennsuco—named for a sugar company that failed. I lived there from birth, 1936, till I was married in 1959. So I grew up heavily influenced by the stories of the Everglades." He goes into a story about the columnist Dave Barry spending a day with him, when Barry was doing a day-in-the-life-of series. The first thing Barry asks him is what is he going to do about the frogs in Florida? There are too many frogs and they're slimy.

"I said, 'Dave, I'm with you on this and I've already done something about it. My backyard was the Everglades. When I was a boy I used to go out there and wait for frogs. It's not easy to get a frog with a BB pellet; it tends to bounce off them. I had to wait for it to croak when it would expose the soft underneck. If you could fire into that area you could get your frog.' Barry was taken aback."

I'm wondering if Graham's connection with the Everglades is anything greater than fond childhood memories of slaughtering frogs but I jump to another subject: "The main idea behind the Comprehensive Plan is that everyone will learn and make changes as the project develops. What about Aquifer Storage and Recovery? There doesn't appear to be much of a contingency plan for if-or-when they don't work."

"I'm not going to go beyond my hydrological knowledge, but if it's found that these underground reservoirs are not the appropriate solution, I guess they'll have to go to larger surface water reservoirs. That will require substantially more land and it won't be as efficient because of the greater evaporation."

"I think there's a lot of debate about evapotranspiration. Wouldn't aboveground reservoirs, or simply returning the old flow to the Everglades, be cheaper than the Aquifer Storage and Recovery system?" I ask.

"If your goal is to have water flow like it did in 1900, then that goal would be inhibited if you had very large surface water reservoirs that evaporated. . . ." he answers, uncomfortably. "But that is a good example of a question that politicians should defer to scientists."

Jumping back to what the Everglades evokes, I talk about how it makes me feel when I'm in it—the peacefulness that overwhelms me—and ask if he's ever felt the same.

"I find spending time in the Everglades to be a very renewing experience, too," he says. "I like the quiet of the Everglades, the relative quiet of nature . . . When I was a boy, the Navy had built a training site near us, and we'd see planes flying overhead often. A not insignificant number of those trainees ended up crashing in the Everglades and my dad was one of the few people with enough knowledge of the area to be able to guide the Navy on rescue missions. I accompanied him on several of those and that is an experience that impressed me with the potential violence of the Everglades. When you're out in all that saw grass and cut off from the rest of the world and generally there aren't any markers. It's kinda intimidating."

I tell him about Hugh Willoughby, the guy who wrote about crossing the Everglades at the end of the nineteenth century, and how he lamented the inevitable changes that would befall the Everglades.

"The Everglades is always changing . . . I'm kinda practicing my speech on you: One of the things I'm going to bring up today is that there isn't a place if you have legitimate concerns regarding the restoration project. For instance, *The Washington Post* had this series of articles on the Everglades this year that I found to be shallow. A lot of the reporting was based on rumors perpetrated by some environmental groups, but if there had been a forum to discuss the reporter's questions then he could've gotten his facts right." He pauses, perhaps giving a second thought. "Anybody who thinks there is an insurance policy that this project will sustain itself for the next twenty years is a very optimistic person."

"Given that, don't you think there should be a review board that has more power—power to tell the Corps they can't do something because it doesn't make scientific sense if the goal is restoration?"

"No, I don't. Congress shouldn't hand over a governmental authority to a nongovernmental entity. On the other hand, if such a group were to present scientific arguments that the Corps isn't doing the correct thing, those of us who do have the political responsibility will be very receptive to it. I believe enough people in Congress understand this idea: that it is not a source of shame to fail one way and then try another."

"So wouldn't you want a board to have that power so these things will get done?"

"In a democracy I believe ultimately that the representatives accountable to the people should be responsible. There are certainly pragmatic reasons enough in history to support giving away this power, but the consequence is that this will further contribute to the deterioration of representational democracy. You might feel you can't trust Congress to mediate between scientific groups that have differing opinions, but that is what Congress is there to do."

Damn. I was really hoping to pin this whole thing on him, make it clear it's his lack of commitment and leadership that has allowed restoration to be sidestepped. That's what I've finally come to believe: The restoration movement has been usurped by a waterworks program. But he's made his point and he's right. Our elected officials—the people we give the power to run our country—should be the ones deciding how things work—not some elite board of scientists who have no allegiance to the people. Only problem with that is most of our elected officials don't have time to study the entire situation. Instead, they often rely on their staff to make their decisions for them, and we don't elect their staff.

We've arrived in Delray Beach and pull into the Marriott Hotel. ("Across the street from the ocean," says his itinerary.) A Hummer is blocking the left side of the check-in lane. A large sign says NO PARKING. "I hate those things," he says, pointing to the Hummer. Graham looks concerned and wonders aloud if they'll let him leave his car with the valet anyway since he's giving the keynote speech. We stand out of the car and a valet jumps through the door, saying, "Senator Graham!" Then he's whisked away by his handlers and surrounded by a handful of Everglades nuts—one wearing a captain's hat, like the Skipper's on *Gilligan's Island*, the other dressed in flowing African garb. Graham looks around to say good-bye, but someone else jumps in his face. And he's gone. Later, during his speech to the coalition audience, he announces that his big agenda for the coming year is getting the Everglades Trail up and running—the driving trail that is supposed to showcase the area's ecology, history, and charm.

He also says he's going to be the next president of the United States.

The Ur-Glades

L IKE MOST PEOPLE, I LIKE TO FIND SOMEBODY TO BLAME.
We're trained as kids that there's always somebody to
pin the problem on. It starts with Daddy stomping
into the kitchen, yelling, "Who did this?" while towering
over the broken bowl, Spaghetti-O's everywhere. Little
Johnny is the only one there, so it's pretty obvious who did
it, but the question is still asked.

It doesn't stop there, of course. It reaches every level
of life, every level of society. Blaming is our national pas-
time, a sport more keenly played and revered than base-
ball.

When you talk to people about the Everglades, those
who want to save it, that is, much of the discourse is about
blame. They spend almost as much energy trying to get

some guilty party to accept responsibility as fighting to bring about change.

But who is to blame for the current state of the Everglades? The Corps, which was just improving what others had started? Who were trying to save lives? Carrying out an assignment given by Congress?

Big Sugar, which is pushed and promoted by our government?

Florida's early American settlers, who were just fulfilling our Manifest Destiny? Who thought it was their duty to drain the swamp?

The Calusa, for having built mounds and levees to preserve their individual lives?

Mother Nature, for taking so long to get around to making the Everglades?

There, it's all their fault. They did it. But, of course, that doesn't solve anything and we already knew that. Others have tried to nail Big Sugar to the Everglades cross, or the Corps, or even the SFWMD. I thought I could lay it all on Graham; he's been around the longest and, by all rights, ought to be able to do something. He was going to be my smoking gun. He and his staff have failed the Everglades repeatedly, while maintaining an image of environmental responsibility. If he had simply pushed for real restoration, more control over the Corps, then the Everglades would stand a chance. Yes, he could have done these things and certainly had the power to do so, given the Water Resources and Development Act which specifically said the Army must come up with a plan to restore the South Florida ecosystem. But he didn't think he had to.

It's not his fault. It's ours. Sometimes we're too damned pragmatic. Too much like Huck Finn, too little like Tom Sawyer.

* * *

And this is what we're left with:

As usual, it's an irrepressibly sunny day in northwest Miami—another mighty fine day for kicking Nature's butt. Luckily, that's not just Chris Zitzow's mission; it's his job: Destroy all water plants that cross his path. Actually, churning down Florida's C-7 (a canal, sometimes known as the Little River, that flows right by Joe Robie Stadium in northern Miami), he's systematically decimating them. Chris roams the waterway in a stubby nine-ton powerboat, a crazed sci-fi killing machine with herky-jerky hydraulic movements and a single-minded ability to fulfill its only purpose: kill, kill, kill. Pitted against Chris and the thousand-pound steel-toothed plow dragged behind his boat, the poor hydrilla, water hyacinth, and pondweed don't stand a chance.

Chris, a thirty-seven-year-old native of Homestead, Florida, kills plants for the South Florida Water Management District (SFWMD), the state agency responsible for keeping Florida's 1800 miles of southern canals flowing. Chris has been operating his nineteen-foot, nine-ton tow boat for a little over a year so that this canal, along with dozens of others, can continue to dump the estimated 1.7 billion gallons of fresh water into the ocean a day—more than three years after the Comprehensive Plan is signed into law. Nothing's changed and nothing will—for years to come. Not that Chris necessarily agrees with the role he's playing. "The Everglades is beautiful, but the way they've messed around with the water, they've ruined it," he says after unloading a pile of water plants onto the eroded bank.

By the time Chris and another plow operator have finished a "reach" (roughly a mile-long section), the plants will have already grown to the surface back at the beginning. Hydrilla and cabomba return the fastest. Pet owners, ridding themselves of dead or simply unloved fish, introduced hydrilla when dumping their tanks into the canals; cabomba is actually native but treated like an invasive species. The SFWMD spends millions of dollars each year, trying to eradicate nonnative plants and animals that threaten not only water flow but also native plant and fish species. Hydrilla, a nonnative species along with water hyacinth, can grow to fifty feet long, cover an acre of water with 135 tons of plant matter, and reproduce from mere shreds. Water hyacinth, decorated with unforgettable lavender flowers, was introduced to Florida by a Mrs. W. F. Fuller of Brooklyn, New York, with a winter home along the Saint Johns. Mrs. Fuller found the floating flowers—a souvenir from the 1884 New Orleans Cotton Exposition—so divine that she felt it was her duty to brighten up the Saint Johns, my friend Brutus the manatee's winter stomping grounds, by transplanting some of her water hyacinth's offspring into the river. Within ten years, water hyacinths covered some 50 million watery acres in Central Florida. The three-foot-long plants form nearly impermeable mats so intertwined that a canal of the hyacinth looks like a flowered roadway.

Hyacinth, hydrilla, and cabomba growth is so thick and jammed up after heavy rainfall that a person can walk across the surface, or so goes the claim. (I wouldn't recommend trying it, considering the things that get pulled out of these canals.) In such times the canals might flood and ruin the eternal development that lines them. To keep this from occurring, the SFWMD employs seventy people year-round, maintains nine towboats, releases hundreds of thousands of grass carp (good for controlling hydrilla), and so many gallons of poison you don't even want to think about it.

Chris spends forty-hour weeks on South Florida's canals making sure the water still flows. He prefers it to working in some office, and these endless sluiceways aren't so bad once you've spent a little time on them. They are sort of like a grubby Everglades theme park. In less than an hour I have seen a ranchful of cattle egrets, a lone burrowing owl trapped in its den by an overturned drywall bucket, enough coots to make a king-sized pillow, a shrieking osprey, half a dozen great blue herons, albeit peering through floating scraps of plastic and paper, and a couple of anhinga drying their wings. More important, Chris has killed a hundred pounds of plants. We've scooped up two basketballs, a bicycle, and a suitcase in the boat's front-end loader—as good as a decent day of Dumpster diving. And the flora, although destined for destruction as soon as we come upon it, is breathtaking. The pink water-lily blooms, bracketed by a rusting shopping cart and discarded beer cans, sweetly complement a pink single-wide a hundred feet up the bank.

Sitting alongside Chris, earplugs in place to minimize the whine of the Detroit 471 engine, I breathe in the rich heady aroma of spent diesel intermingled with foul, over-ripe ditch water, and I know, without a doubt, that I have finally found the heart of the Everglades—now and forever.

You can do it all in the canals: fish, dump your trash, watch birds (I saw more species of wildlife in the one day I rode in Chris's towboat than anywhere else), and perhaps even get rid of unwanted neighbors; Chris recently found a car manned by someone who'd been missing for five years. Once the Comprehensive Plan is implemented, you'll be able to do all of this in the canals, while simultaneously feeling as if you're part of the natural world, in a Disney kind of way. On your left, you might find man-made hammocks with reintroduced native deer, cypresses, and manmade swamps housing fattened alligators. On your right, perhaps a Florida cougar, genetically cloned, will lurk among the saw grass, waiting for your baby to fall overboard. And if federally mandated filters work, the noxious agricultural runoff water will even appear pristine.

The canals might look less natural than ex-Senate-majority-leader Lott's hairdo, but nonetheless, they are the arteries, the lifeblood even, for the current Everglades and its vibrant new future. To put it another way, they hold the Everglades by the cojones and under our $8 billion restoration plan, this will not change.

Most of the canals that currently discharge all that life-giving freshwater into the ocean will simply be rerouted to the new wells, the still unproven underground reservoirs injected from the surface. Others will be reshaped and widened, not necessarily to appear more natural, although they will be dotted with little islands and freshly planted indigenous trees, but so that more water can skirt the sugarcane farms, saving them from flood and ruin. The ur-canals will be a recreationer's paradise—a stop-and-shop subtropical car-camping paradise, with plenty of put-ins, concrete boat ramps, and septic tank disposal areas. All brought to you by the makers of the lovely lower Mississippi, the stagnant Columbia River, and the superhighway once known as the Missouri River. This time, though, there won't be any mistakes. Ur-levees with impervious barriers will be raised to keep the water in these new riverlike canals, and when water does seep out into a canal on the other side, massive pumps will send it right back where it came from.

And no matter what, this will be the Everglades. So, despite what we like to tell ourselves, despite what we may wish for, no one—not the manatees, not the coral, not the snail kites, not the mosquito fish—can go home again.

I Am Florida

I S THAT ALL WE HAVE TO LOOK FORWARD TO?
It's November. It's already cold in Maine. It looks as if we're going to have the worst winter in decades. I've heard about this place in Florida where things look like they did 500 years ago. It's warm there. The sun shines but it doesn't reveal grime or dead manatees; it sparkles on pristine waters. Fish and sharks and turtles and fun are everywhere. It's the Dry Tortugas.

And, I'm thinking, any fool living in Maine given half a chance would seize the opportunity to sail with his family in the Florida Keys in November, especially if he's been traveling down there for three years in a row usually without that same family. Any fool, even if his wife is seven months pregnant and has only been out of the hospital for a week since suffering a near deadly case of bacterial meningitis, and her doctors are telling her she absolutely cannot leave the state. Even if this is his crew: Helen, now age five, dark-haired, blue-eyed hellcat whose fondest desire is to own a live pig; Anabel and Eliza, six-year-old twin acrobats with no understanding of the word *no*. Even if he's moved four times in eight months while people did unspeakable and unaffordable things to his home. And even if he'll be guiding a thirty-six-foot sybaritic catamaran seventy miles off-shore with just a modicum of captaining experience so his family can fulfill his personal desire to find an untouched corner of the Everglades.

We're talking the Dry Tortugas, the very last stretch of the Everglades ecosystem. Even the name sounds exotic. Ponce de León provisioned his expedition with hundreds of *Tortugas,* turtles, when he came upon these keys in 1513, and they're called dry because they hold no fresh water. The Dry Tortugas have been a national park for just ten years and are mostly unused, except by sailors and a few tarpon-chasing sportfishermen who don't count since all they ever seem to remember is the whopper that got away. More birds travel through the Dry Tortugas than any other spot in the U.S. Rookeries abound throughout the park.

Vibrant, colorful reefs and wrecked ships lie a mere five feet beneath the surface, almost as if they've been placed there for little kids to snorkel around and see more fish than they ever imagined. Even the guy who chartered me the boat agrees: "There's no finer place in Florida for snorkeling," he boasts. "You're gonna love it."

I have a theory that the place looks like Florida Bay used to—that turtle grass here is as common as saw grass is back on the river. I'm going to swim between those flat blades of life-sustaining vegetation, and for once I'm going to feel all right.

I create a goal for our family—reach Fort Jefferson, sitting seventy miles out to sea. What kid doesn't like a fort, even if, as in this case, the fort is near collapse?

So we go down to Florida one last time, scraping together frequent flyer miles, escaping our troubles, taking on a little adventure. If you don't count the $144 speeding ticket unduly inflicted upon me for being an out-of-stater in a construction zone without evidence of any construction (never mind that it was also a "Key Deer Protection Area"— no one but the tiny key deer could see those tiny signs), the first night on our boat, docked at the Oceanside Marina, goes pretty well, all in all. What with traveling all day, the ticket, the unmade beds upon our 10:00 P.M. arrival, the stench of urine that wafts from the bilge like a lonely cloud of skunk musk, and an endless series of dreams in which I wreck planes and cars, fight monsters and armies, and watch my whole world destroyed, I am feeling fine the next morning when the girls wake up at six.

You see, I've never chartered such a big boat in my entire, short history of sailing. I've done some extreme sailing and have captained my own twenty-three-foot boat in a number of sticky situations with the children on board, but I've never been in charge of a thirty-six-foot boat and sailed it day after day. Let's face it: I'm afraid. And, even worse, I can't show it. I've told Lisa I can handle the boat, that I'm not worried a bit, and I've convinced the charter company that I'm a capable, responsible seaman.

All of this—the speeding ticket, the fear, the bravado— it's all to be expected. It is during Robin's (partner with John in Southernmost Sailing Boat Charters) precharter talk that our voyage takes an unforeseen tack. Her bit about vessels overtaking us or our running aground? Not a problem. I'm not gonna let that happen. I'm Captain Everglades!

All changes, though, when she uses the *P* word. Yachtsmen love to bandy this word about. It's a verbal secret-society handshake and is the antithesis of my very being. But Robin uses it and that is that. "This time of year with the sun setting so quickly it'd be *prudent* to anchor by four. It pays to be *prudent*. Speaking of which, your plan to reach the Dry Tortugas? Not *prudent*. You simply don't have enough time. You have a new boat you don't know. You have an area you've never sailed. You're here to have fun, and if you bite off more than you can chew, it's no fun anymore and the whole point is to have fun." Hmmm.

"Did you hear that, Hodding?" Lisa asks.

"In the past, I've had a problem with prudency. . . ."

"That's not a word, Hodding," Lisa helps.

"Um, being prudent. Hey, I've made up a word."

"That's a good thing," Robin says, smiling, "because the English language is short on words."

Ha, ha.

"Hey," she continues, "as long as you're good at making up words, maybe you could help me. I've been trying to come up with a word for three years now that means, 'good idea, bad execution.' "

"Well," I offer, "how about, 'you pulled a Hodding'?"

"Naw, I think it needs to be a little more universal than that."

Robin is not what I imagined a representative from a charter company to be like. She's smart. She's bright. She keeps me in my place.

I ask her about seeing staghorn coral. A friend has told me there's some great staghorn over by Fort Jefferson.

"The staghorn is not in plentiful supply, but there are a couple of places that still have some," she answers. The whole place used to be forested with the stuff. I tell her I think the place should be called the Largest Dead Coral Reef.

"It's not that bad," she answers. "We have a wonderful nonprofit organization here called Reef Relief that does a good job on education which I think is the most important thing for protecting the coral. They put out mooring buoys by the reefs so you don't have to drop an anchor. The problem is that the buoys are difficult to see because being a non-profit organization, Reef Relief bought the cheapest, smallest buoys possible."

Shouldn't somebody be doing more than just frowning? It's supposed to be a federally protected reef.

"The main problem is education," she continues. "People don't realize that coral is alive. It's an animal, not a rock. If you touch it, it will die. If you smack it really hard, like with a boat, of course it dies faster, but if you just touch it, it dies an agonizing death because the grease in your hands is poison to them."

I tell her one of the reasons we're here is that the Keys and the Dry Tortugas could be seen as the furthest extent of the Everglades.

"Yeah, well, water quality is a big issue," she says. "When I first moved here fifteen years ago, everyone would say, 'Oh, the water used to be much clearer.' Well, you can't have thirty thousand people living year-round on a four-and-a-half-mile island without some environmental impact. We started studying the pollution, and at first everybody thought it was mostly from the passing boats and cruise ships. We get dozens and dozens of cruise ships here every month. But what we discovered is that our sewage system was old and in disrepair and was leeching into the ocean because our water table is just a few feet below the surface. We voted, put a bond in place, and doubled our sewer bills so we could spend three years replacing every inch of our sewers. Every inch. Recently, we've gone back and tested the lateral line to each house and building and made sure each building owner replaced the lines that leaked. About 25 percent have needed to do so."

After she's done with us, her partner John takes over. His job? Make us comfortable with the boat. We go over everything in detail—the massive electronics, battery charge maintenance, emergency pull-cords for the twin outboard motors, water systems, head pumps, refrigeration, sails, anchors. He talks for more than an hour. I probably soak up ten minutes worth. To his credit, he barely flinches when Helen and Eliza drop thirty CDs on his head as he's showing me the electronics board.

Near the end of his talk, as the girls are pestering me to swim off the stern with them (and where I think we've been emptying our head all morning), four manatees rise a few yards away.

"Manatees!" I scream out.

"Girls, girls," Lisa calls. "Manatees are coming."

They slowly swim straight for us. "BRUTUS!" all three girls yell. "It's BRUTUS, Mommy. Daddy, it's BRUTUS!"

"No, no. That's not Brutus, girls," I say, although I'm just as excited as they are. How in the name of hell do I know if that's Brutus or not? I can't remember what Brutus's scar looks like, and one of these manatees is big enough to be him and has a big fat scar on its back. I guess I still don't want it to be, hoping that he's hiding under protest until we get our act in gear.

"Helen, can you believe it?" Eliza says as our girls run along the boat's deck, following the manatees as they swim toward our bow.

"No, I didn't know they'd be here," Helen says. She was

a little over two when we went down to see Brutus. Now she's five. Anabel is silent. She's following them like she's a hound dog—a trained manatee watcher.

We hop off the boat and go running down the dock. Robin joins us. She seems just as excited. "They look pretty good," she says. "Not too many scars."

Suddenly a boat is coming out of a canal straight in front of us on a head-on collision course for all four manatees. Robin sprints down to the end of the dock, waving her arms frantically, high in the air. "There's MANATEES!" she screams. "SLOW DOWN. MANATEES!" She points down to the water.

The man hears and sees her. He cuts his engine to a near idle. Meanwhile, the manatees have dropped deeper beneath the surface. She's given them enough time to escape another hit.

"If she hadn't been here, that guy would've hit the manatees," Lisa says. "Do you think that was Brutus?"

Five hours later, we are sailing downwind in a rolling sea as blue and blissful as my wife's suddenly sparkling eyes. Robin has suggested we go only a few miles the first day and sail around to Key West's old port, but we set our sights on Boca Grande Key about eighteen miles out to sea. From there it will be an easy two-day sail to Fort Jefferson, stopping on the way to snorkel at a shipwreck a friend said we shouldn't miss. We are making seven knots, the skies are clear, and everyone is smiling. Never mind that one of the boat's two twenty-five-hp engines is already nonfunctioning. It doesn't matter. The natural world has blessed our fleet with the arrival of those manatees.

We are bound for the Dry Tortugas, where children turn angelic and parents feel at peace.

We reach Boca Grande an hour before sunset, anchoring safely on the leeward, northwest shore. It's an unusual anchorage for the Keys in that the water remains deep— some eighteen feet—just a few feet from the shore. Even I can't run aground. In many areas in the Keys the water can be a foot deep a mile out.

Also, Boca Grande has a shore out of your earliest dreams of a fantasy island—a beautiful white beach that curves into a bordering forest of mangroves. Great white egrets and a Helen-sized osprey watch us struggle with the anchor. A gentle wind whirs in the rigging, harmless ripples lap our hulls. Mullets leap like shimmering Baryshnikovs above the surface and disappearing into the horizon. I'm thrilled that we've started out so anti-prudent and sailed all this way to the anchorage of hope.

Most of Boca Grande is a wildlife refuge, with NO TRES- PASSING signs clearly marking where not to go. We go ashore in the burnished glow of dusk on the edge of the protected land. Horseshoe crabs clumsily hide from our splashing feet. Stingrays stealth into the sandy bottom, and the girls learn that sponges aren't always fluorescent rectangles manufactured for washing dishes, but actual living crea- tures. Dozens lie washed up on shore, looking like some politically minded art installation, scattered among shiny Coke and beer cans and scraps of multicolored plastic. So much for my belief that this area will be pristine. Flotsam is inescapable.

Anabel keeps one of the conical sponges as a hat.

Later, we sit on our boat's trampoline, watching stars fall from the sky, giggling with relief that things are good.

The next day we sail on to the Marquesas, a ring of islands eight miles west with a shallow interior haunted by a fringe of mangroves. Mangroves fringe nearly everything down here, just as they once did nearly all of South Florida. Downtown Miami? Mangroves. Naples? Mangroves.

My plan is for us to spend the afternoon there, snorkeling by a shipwreck and studying a frigate bird rookery, and then head across to the Dry Tortugas at night. The tradewinds, I reckon, will fetch us to the southwestern side of the Marquesas in a little over an hour. Leaving the Marquesas once the children are asleep at 9:00 P.M., we can be anchored beside Fort Jefferson by 4:00 A.M. I let Lisa in on my thoughts.

"Are you crazy? Didn't they tell us not to go there? What happened with being prudent?" she asks pleasantly enough, uttering the *P* word for the first time since we left Oceanside Marina. At the moment she says this she is also studying the chart to make sure we don't smash into some shallows (I am sailing within a hundred yards of them at seven knots) so I can't tell if she's really about to kill me.

"Coming about!" I yell. She jumps up, hauls in the starboard sheet and, huffing like a mama bear, turns her full attention toward me. She's been a little miffed with me all morning, ever since I had her trying to raise the mainsail when I still had the halyard clipped to the deck. The exertion, intensified by my screaming, "Lisa, get it up. Get it up!" almost caused her pregnant body to pass out.

"Are you thinking about the children?"

"I can handle this boat, sweetie," I answer and then see that something is amiss. The sails stall, the jib backs, and then we're headed toward the rocks again. "Let the sheet go! We didn't make it." We fall off the wind, speed up, try to come about and fail to make it once more. Lisa stands there, aghast.

I cut on the remaining good engine. It catches, but something is wrong. It only notches us up a knot or so, barely enough to help us cross the wind but no aid in getting us anywhere. We spend the next four hours trying to get a mile upwind with the girls asking when we're going to swim and when we're going to get there every five minutes. We don't anchor until just shy of sunset.

By this time the girls are crying for that swim but won't go in unless I do. Lisa isn't really talking to me.

I don't know what to do. This isn't going as planned. I'm mad at myself. I'm frustrated. I am Florida.

I have to do something right. So I jump. I sail over the deck. I imagine I am suspended in midair. Maybe the magnificent frigate bird, the air pirate of the western Keys, will swoop down and take me away. But, of course, I just plunge down, down into the dark green waters.

But when I land . . . when I land everything changes. There's something down here. Some papery strands scratching my arms, my legs and torso. It's like nothing I've felt before. I'm entangled in . . . turtle grass. The entire ocean floor appears to be covered with turtle grass. I stay down there for as long as I can, twisting and turning in the flat strands like an ecstatic manatee, coming up only when my lungs force me to surface.

"Daddy!" the girls scream out. "Oh, Daddy!" And they jump, one by one, plunging into our very own fountain of youth.

A few minutes later Lisa joins us, gently easing herself into the water. She floats toward me.

"You know I love adventures, Hodding. If it were just us . . . but maybe you're right. I'm not . . ." she begins.

"No, no. You're right. I can't sail that thing well enough. Let's stay here. This is it. It's what we were looking for anyway."

An empty Coke can floats by, and I do my best to ignore it.

The Beginning

I WENT INTO THE EVERGLADES KNOWING NOTHING AND NOW I know at least one thing. I know that the Everglades is supposed to be a river, although the public's never been able to grasp that notion, despite Marjorie Stoneman Douglas and all the literature that's followed her lovely book. And by the time certain people realized it was a river, we'd already turned it into a swamp.

I also believe I know what we should do if we really want to restore it.

This won't take long. It's really very easy; the wackos have been suggesting it for decades. Do the one, and only one, thing that works in this country when we want to preserve an environment. Make the entire historic Everglades a national park—from Lake Okeechobee on down to

Florida Bay. Get rid of this half-assed solution called the Comprehensive Plan and revamp Everglades National Park. The latter is a disgrace—a once bucolic, natural setting, now reduced to scraping by on the leavings of industry, and the former, while well intentioned, is a gutless compromise that has nothing to do with the original congressional request to *restore* the Everglades.

Congress didn't say pat the Everglades on the back. It didn't say give it a blue-blooded, penny-pinching handout. It didn't tell the Florida legislature to kick it in the butt while wearing a big Bozo-the-Clown smile on its face. It said RESTORE the damned Everglades, and Congress said this because that's what we said we wanted. So give us what we want.

Big Sugar? Kick 'em out. They've had their day. I'm all for people making money but not at my expense. Adjust the Sugar Program so that it only helps needy farmers and see how fast those fat cats flee. Then buy out the smaller farmers. They only own 10 percent of the land. Let's help out Brazil, our neighbor and ally, by buying their cheap sugar. Brazil is the world's leading producer and we don't buy a single pound, despite its cheaper price.

Clewiston, America's Sweetest Town? I'd say move it. Less than seven thousand people live there. We've moved that many people when building dikes and dams elsewhere. Why not do the same when dismantling one? The towns southeast and southwest of the lake could be protected with some of the Corps' nifty new impervious levees; everything else between is either sugarcane fields or Clewiston. And if we don't have the will to move Clewiston, which I admit is a bit of a stretch, why not at least buy out most of the farms? Then we'd get some real restoration—a twenty-mile-wide space for sheet flow.

Soil subsidence? Fill it back in. Unlike those Aquifer Storage and Recovery systems, we know filling-in works. Look at how simple saving the Kissimmee has been, and that's just one big plow job. Put me in a big yellow Caterpillar and I'll do the job. Hell, even my six-month-old son could do it with his beach shovel. And if that's going too far, then let time fill it back in. Biological deposits and the southwest tilt of the Florida Plateau will take care of the subsidence issue.

The coastal cities? Build your better levees along the eastern and western perimeters to protect them and then get the hell out of there. If you let the Everglades flow, their drinking water will be continually replenished. And it will be clean. Which reminds me, the Everglades isn't simply some touchy-feely issue about a bunch of birds; it's also about providing safe, clean drinking water. And the natural Everglades is one of the best water filters in the world. SO here's a concept: Let's provide the citizens of Miami and the tourists who visit South Florida with naturally clean water, instead of the filtered sludge of the Sugar Industry's leavings.

Tamiami Trail? Raise it—all of it. It'll be the mother of all causeways stretching from the outskirts of Miami to downtown Naples and could be renamed the Everglades Freeway. A showcase of American civil engineering.

It's this simple: Finish cleaning the headwaters up north, allow Okeechobee to spill over with new, fresh water, and let the river flow.

After all, isn't this what we think we're paying for?

Further Reading

Instead of listing all the books and articles I read while reporting this book, I've selected those I found most useful and/or enjoyable.

Bartram, William. *Travels though North and South Carolina, Georgia, East and West Florida.* Philadelphia, 1791. Reprint, New York: Dover Publications, 1928.

Didion, Joan. *Miami.* New York: Dover Publications, 1987.

Douglas, Marjorie. *The Everglades: River of Grass.* New York: Rinehart, 1947. Reprint, Sarasota, Florida: Pineapple Press, 1997.

Henshall, James A. *Camping and Cruising in Florida.* Cincinnati, 1884. Reprint, Port Salerno, Florida: Florida Classics Library, 1991.

Hiaasen, Carl. *Strip Tease.* New York: Warner Books, 1994.

Matthiessen, Peter. *Killing Mr. Watson.* New York: Random House, 1990.

McCally, David. *The Everglades: An Environmental History.* Gainesville, Florida: University Press of Florida, 1999.

Mintz, Sidney W. *Sweetness and Power.* New York: Viking, 1985.

Romans, Bernard. *A Concise Natural History of East and West Florida.* New York, 1775. Reprint, New Orleans: Pelican Publishing, 1961.

Rothchild, John. *Up for Grabs.* New York: Viking, 1985.

Smith, Buckingham. *Report of Buckingham Smith, Esq.* 30th Congress, 1st session, 1848.

Tebeau, Charlton W. *Man in the Everglades.* Coral Gables: University of Miami Press, 1968.

Vignoles, Charles. *Observations Upon the Floridas.* New York, 1823.

Wilkinson, Alec. *Big Sugar.* New York: Knopf, 1989.

Willoughby, Hugh. *Across the Everglades.* Philadelphia, 1898. Reprint, Port Salerno, Florida: Florida Classics Library, 1992.

Acknowledgments

Thanks to:

Steve Robinson, for sharing his time, passion, and back porch

Phyllis Neuhart, for organizing the wonkfests at the Knight Foundation

Megan Waters, for finding everything needed when called upon at Florida International University's online Everglades library

Alan Farago, for trying to make me understand

Elizabeth Hightower, for sending me out there

Russell Kaye, for suffering with me once again (and loaning his photos)

Bill Graf, for going beyond his SFWMD duties and making a damned-good dinner

261

Acknowledgments

Saranne Taylor, for boosting morale in the Everglades

David Conover, for his sage advice and unswerving willingness to be a foil

The Florida Legislature, for making so many dumb decisions these past few years, thus giving me more to write about

The mermaids at Weeki Wachee, for being there

Sally Wofford Girand, for being a tenacious agent and good friend

Judith Curr, for her watery vision and faith

Luke Dempsey, for being such a needling, endearing editor

Wendy Walker, for her production follow-through

My mom, for making me curious

My dad, for his insightful reading and comments

Patt, for her open-door policy

My wife, Lisa, for her unflinching view of Florida and my writing

Brutus, for never showing up

Index